Leadership Lessons
from Jesus

Leadership Lessons from Jesus

Guidance We Have Missed
from His Actions and Words

DOREEN M. McFARLANE

WIPF & STOCK · Eugene, Oregon

LEADERSHIP LESSONS FROM JESUS
Guidance We Have Missed from His Actions and Words

Copyright © 2025 Doreen M. McFarlane. All rights reserved. Except for brief quotations in critical publications or reviews, no part of this book may be reproduced in any manner without prior written permission from the publisher. Write: Permissions, Wipf and Stock Publishers, 199 W. 8th Ave., Suite 3, Eugene, OR 97401.

Wipf & Stock
An Imprint of Wipf and Stock Publishers
199 W. 8th Ave., Suite 3
Eugene, OR 97401

www.wipfandstock.com

PAPERBACK ISBN: 979-8-3852-4905-3
HARDCOVER ISBN: 979-8-3852-4906-0
EBOOK ISBN: 979-8-3852-4907-7

VERSION NUMBER 05/07/25

Unless otherwise noted, Scripture quotations are from the New Revised Standard Version Updated Edition, copyright © 2021 National Council of the Churches of Christ in the United States of America. Used by permission. All rights reserved worldwide.

This book is affectionately dedicated to the memory of one beloved professor who so patiently took the time to guide his students at the Lutheran School of Theology at Chicago: the late Walter Michel. May he rest in peace, and may his memory be a blessing to all of us who so fondly remember him.

Contents

Introduction | ix

Chapter I: Leaders as Good Communicators | 1
Chapter II: Leaders as Their Best Selves | 24
Chapter III: Leaders Deal with Change | 50
Chapter IV: Leaders Deal with the Negative | 59
Chapter V: Leaders Deal with Enemies | 74
Chapter VI: Leaders Deal with Assets | 83
Chapter VII: Leaders Encourage Others | 96
Chapter VIII: Leaders Move Forward | 109

Conclusion | 121
Bibliography | 125

Introduction

WHETHER YOU ARE A CEO right now, another type of leader, or you sense the call to leadership, you have probably asked yourself, "What do I have to do to be a dynamic and courageous leader?" We all want courageous leaders in our workplaces, business institutions, religious establishments, political organizations, and governments. But, as we have observed, a genuinely good leader is hard to find. Those who are chosen to lead undoubtedly have many qualities. Still, we are often disappointed in the behavior of many who lead us. Were our hopes for them too high? Were they good to begin with and later corrupted in some way by power? Is excellent and courageous leadership even possible? Three questions come to mind. What constitutes a good leader? How can a person (you?) become such a leader? And how can leaders be true to their calling and continue to improve their leadership skills?

The goal of this book is to consider such questions by taking a close look at the courageous leadership of Jesus. For this book, Jesus' own leadership (as he is presented by the Gospel writers) will serve as the benchmark. (As this is not intended to be a scholarly book, distinctions will not be made between the particular texts of the Synoptic Gospels [Matthew, Mark, and Luke] and the quite different and, shall we say, more liturgical Gospel of John, which is believed to have been written considerably later. For the purpose of studying leadership, this book examines the words and acts of Jesus as historical accounts rather than created or redacted [edited] narratives.)

Of course, Jesus wasn't exactly a CEO per se because his goals were much higher than just to be successful in business. Still, his life and actions were such that his message remains as alive after over two thousand years as it was from the beginning. People continue to follow him. Whether we are CEOs already or beginners, wouldn't leading like Jesus be too high a goal for us then? Well, maybe, but then why not learn from the best?

In our times, we have no shortage of popular books offering new and dynamic leadership strategies. This book is not one of them. It is also not a devotional book or even a specifically "religious" or "spiritual" book. So, why the choice of Jesus? First, his life and work offer the world a model for responsible and dynamic leadership, whether those who study his life are Christians or not. Second, leadership often brings up issues of ethics and morality and again, of course, Jesus leads the way. Third, most people, both Christian and non-Christian, have an interest in the life and words of Jesus. Jesus was honest, open, and without guile. He meant what he said, spoke with authority, led without fear, and he even knew when to remain silent. His courage in the face of adversity serves as a primary model for the courage we seek to be genuine leaders. His integrity in all that he did presents us with the consummate role model. Jesus, as we know him through the Gospels, continually and consistently demonstrates outstanding leadership.

This book offers examples from the life and teachings of Jesus, as practical as any can be; a guide to the best kind of leadership. The leadership lessons presented here, far from being out of date, prove to be practical and useful for our contemporary lives and for our leadership in this complex and diverse twenty-first-century world. Each section of the book presents a leadership challenge and offers

THE TEACHABLE MOMENT

For any number of reasons, there are times when we are open to learn and many more when we are not. Jesus had the gift of knowing exactly when "the teachable moment" had come, both for individuals and gathered groups, for friends as well as for enemies. This will be repeatedly demonstrated in the chapters that follow. This book has been written for those who want to pick it up and peruse it when they find themselves in that "teachable" frame of mind. It is also for those who will want to read it straight through, consider the big picture, and then go out and take action, step-by-step, toward a stronger and more courageous leadership. Some of Jesus' leadership ways will be easy to follow and others more challenging.

THE PERSON OF JESUS

Before we proceed, it's good to remind ourselves that Jesus was, of course, a first-century Jewish man who was born, grew to manhood, and died under Roman occupation. As a good Jew, he would have been raised from childhood with some knowledge of the Hebrew Bible, which includes calls to courageous leadership that are a vital part of Jewish Scripture (that which Christians call the Old Testament). Just as one example, in the first chapter of the book of Joshua, God speaks to Joshua about how to behave in the promised land. God tells Joshua, "Be strong and courageous, for you shall lead this people to possess the land that I swore to their ancestors to give them" (Josh 1:6). It goes on to say, "I hereby command you: Be strong and courageous; do not be frightened or dismayed, for the Lord your God is with you wherever you go" (verse 9). Jesus would have been familiar with these and other words of encouragement. Aside from the many stories of Jesus' kindness and gentleness, the New Testament of the Bible offers numerous narratives in which Jesus shows himself to be a brave, authoritative, and commanding leader. He also, on numerous occasions, admonishes the people, "Do not be afraid."

The biblical Jesus is ever ready to challenge us; toss out our ideas of maintaining the "status quo"; push, and sometimes even rush, us on to new horizons. The Jesus who emerges from the written text is a strong leader, willing to demand of us more than we think we have to offer. In this regard he can be seen as a dynamic motivational leader! Jesus is quick of wit, ready and willing to speak out to anyone who is not living out the reign of God right now! Jesus is much more than some "Mr. Nice Guy." In many instances, he seems disrespectful of authority, but it is always in the name of justice. He obeys his boss! He answers to a higher power. His demands of us, of course, are not demands we can always so easily fulfill. It is hoped that, by looking at these texts directly and examining them for their profound leadership messages, readers will hear the strong voice of Jesus the CEO across the millennia, guiding and challenging all of us who truly desire to serve with integrity as faithful and genuinely courageous leaders.

THE JESUS COMMUNITY

The times in which Jesus lived, as well as the later years when the Gospels were being written, were not easy for the Jewish or for the early Christian people. Even though our modern lives are very different, and we are separated from these stories by over two thousand years, there is much to be learned from the words and acts of Jesus which can be directly applied today to our ways of engaging in leadership. Human nature doesn't change that much. Jesus lived in a time of oppression and even of terror, although not exactly the kind of terror we deal with today. The Jewish people suffered under the yoke of Rome's power, often burdened with overtaxation and unfair courts. They lived in continuous personal danger to themselves and those they loved. The Jesus narratives call us to courageous leadership, not just in good times but in times of trial.

INTRODUCTION

They call us also to practical behavior in the face of enemies, and to a love of community in the face of suffering.

The Gospels were written approximately between the year 70 and up to as late as 110 of the Common Era (CE). The decade leading up to the year 70 was a time of great turmoil and war for the Jewish people in and around Jerusalem. In 70, the beloved Jerusalem temple was destroyed by the Romans, and the Jews were removed from their homes and from the city of Jerusalem. The Gospels were written during and after that very painful time, when so many people had lost their place of worship, their homes, jobs, possessions, dignity, and just about everything that had set the core of their religious and ethnic identity. Where did a Jewish person worship without the temple? How did one conduct oneself without the usual religious leaders in place? With the temple gone, the very person of Jesus became the new epicenter of faith for those who chose to believe him the Messiah and to follow what was known as "the Way." Jesus the Christ became their leader, the center of their faith, even more after his death and the belief in his resurrection—with a leadership so authoritative and authentic that this leadership continues to be a living reality in the churches and every place where two or three Christians are gathered together in his name to this day!

READY TO BEGIN!

Those of us who are leaders or "would-be" leaders know, of course, that we are no Jesus! In this book we will be looking at Jesus the man (who, according to the writer of Phil 2:7, "emptied himself" of all divinity and lived as a human like us). Whatever our varying theologies may be regarding his identity, all of us can learn from Jesus. As we look at how he modeled courageous leadership throughout his own ministry and human life, we find we cannot go wrong if we seek to be more like him. None of us is perfect, but every step we take in the directions he taught and modeled will lead us into good places.

Chapter I

Leaders as Good Communicators

To begin, let's look at some of the skills Jesus used as a communicator. If we want to be dynamic leaders, we need to continually be honing our communication skills. The ability to get our points across, to interact with the ideas of others, and to get along with people are all of primary importance for good leadership.

GET THEM TO FOLLOW (JOHN 1:35–51): JESUS GATHERS HIS TEAM

First, we need people who believe in our goals and hopes and dreams, and who are willing to follow us! How do we get them to come along, and, once they've joined our "team," how do we convince them to stay? They won't be willing or interested unless, from the outset, they have confidence in our ability to lead. Some techniques can be learned. Ultimately, our leadership must be authentic and our words sincere. Your leadership will, of course, have to be for everyone's good, not just your own. The goals will need to be those you believe in with all your heart. When this is the case, those who follow you will very likely be caught up in the same dream, and you will work together toward the same results.

The first chapter of the Gospel of John offers a story of how Jesus gathered his primary team, the disciples. Much of John, including this narrative, is written in a very formal, almost liturgical, style, so it is not easy at first to see that it yields so many practical lessons about gathering your people. What did Jesus do or say that got a group of fishermen to literally drop everything and go with him? What was so appealing to them? The religious answer is, of course, that he was, after all, the Son of God, so why wouldn't they want to follow him? But the story also reveals some surprisingly useful and practical leadership tips: skills we can use today to help us attract a really good team.

Be Where the Action Is

This scene opens in a place called Bethany across the Jordan River, where John had been baptizing. For this reason, it can be assumed that the people who have gathered there are people with curiosity who've come looking for something new, maybe even seeking some kind of dynamic change in their lives.

Be Interested in Them

At the outset, Jesus' true identity as "the lamb of God" (John 1:29) is said to have been proclaimed aloud by John the Baptist. Jesus' response to this amazing accolade is silence. It appears he has chosen at this point to neither refute nor agree with any lofty titles John has bestowed on him. When Jesus does speak, he doesn't say one word about himself. Instead, he expresses his interest in those people who are standing around. He begins by asking them a rather strange and open-ended question: "What are you looking for?" (verse 38). It could mean as little as, "To what (geographical) location are you heading right now?" or "Are you lost and looking for directions?" On the other hand, it could be as profound and pithy a question as "What is the direction of your life? Are you looking for a change?" They don't answer directly but they do call him *rabbi* ("teacher"), probably realizing that anyone who would come up with this sort of question must be some kind of teacher! No doubt, their curiosity is aroused. They want to know more! So, now, they ask him a question, a similar question. They want to know where he is staying. Jesus responds, again, not with an answer, but this time with an open invitation: "Come and see" (verse 39). This, again, could mean anything! He has sparked interest. They accept!

See Their Potential and Tell Them So Up Front

Andrew has been interested enough by this time to go and bring his brother, Simon, to meet Jesus, so the group is getting larger. When Jesus takes the trouble of giving Simon (whom he has just met) a new name, announcing that he is now to be called Cephas (verse 42, also Peter), Simon is in! We know from later stories that this man, sometimes known as Simon Peter, tends to act a little bit insecure at times and at other times to act too hastily, so he is very likely thrilled to meet someone who chooses to give him a name that means "rock." Although he often behaves like anything but a rock, it is Simon Peter who'll turn out to be the principal disciple upon whom the church itself will be built.

Make Your Invitation Personal

The next day, Jesus is in Galilee where he meets up with a man named Philip. Jesus uses yet another method to bring Philip into the group. He offers a simple and personal invitation to follow him. Philip accepts.

Appeal to Their Sense of Adventure: Make the Project Enticing

Philip, in turn, brings Nathanael. (Note how it's not Jesus who goes out and gets new disciples. It is those he has chosen who do most of the recruiting.) Jesus gets into a quick and witty conversation with Nathanael, thereby gathering him into the group. Jesus offers him a compliment (possibly a backhanded compliment, to challenge the bright young man). He calls Nathanael an Israelite who is without deceit. Jesus also entices Nathanael by saying that, if he follows him, he will get to see much more than he could ever have imagined. The excitement is mounting. Who could resist? Nathanael is in! (See more about Jesus' encounter with Nathanael in the section "Dealing with Others' Talent" in chapter 7.)

In the above few verses, we can discern five different practical recruiting methods that Jesus has used for attracting and bringing in followers, each method quite different. Here is the list. He deflects focus from his own personality, shows sincere interest in others (as individuals) and in their intentions, and offers an open invitation to learn about the work that is ahead. He lifts them up, seeing them as strong and valuable, and he demonstrates a willingness to engage them in further and more intense dialogue, challenge, and adventure as they move forward together. This seems a worthy recruitment system for any leader today.

There are many ways to attract people to your cause, group, party, place of worship, or business. The above provides an excellent beginning. Your cause or goal itself has to be the focus, not your own personality or charisma, although it may provide an additional plus. Always start with the people you want to lead. Your first interest is in meeting their needs. This is only because, if it does not look like your goals, your cause, or your business will serve their interests as well, especially at the beginning, these people are not likely to join you, or to stay with you for long. Even though you don't talk about yourself, it will still be necessary to clearly articulate the purposes and values of the cause for which you will all be working together. And you'll need to continue with a real interest in your people throughout the whole time you work together. Your genuine concern for and approval of their work when it is truly earned will mean a lot to them. Everyone longs for ongoing support and blessing. As you lift them up, you and they will grow together. First, you will share experiences, probably some failures, then successes, and, for sure, memories. Finally, you and those who follow you will come to understand each other and really be a team as you work together toward those common goals.

Jesus' disciples were simple fishermen. According to some Gospel texts (many in the Gospel of Mark), they often misunderstood him, his work, and words. Yet, after they no longer had his physical presence in this world, it was this same group who found the courage to create and build the church, to preach and heal on his behalf, to face grave danger, and even to be willing to die for his name's sake. Jesus had recognized their potential from the beginning. He knew exactly how to recruit them. And he had not been wrong about them.

Good Leaders

- often choose their followers for their specific talents;
- show an interest and ask good questions;
- focus on others and not themselves;
- offer an open invitation to learn more about themselves and their work;
- support and bless others, seeing them as strong and valuable;
- demonstrate a willingness to engage in further and more intense dialogue.

SET THE AGENDA (MARK 1:16–20): JESUS GIVES THE JOB DESCRIPTION

Employees, team or committee members, or colleagues may be great and talented people. Still, without understanding what they are supposed to be reaching for, their talents may go unused. It is astonishing to think how many people head out to work every day without really knowing their purpose or having clear and workable goals. Too often, with new employees or recently gathered teams, it is assumed that they will simply know what to do once they start working. If the agenda for the individuals, team or group, is understood, then these people will be freed up to move forward in appropriate and hopefully also in creative ways.

Jesus offers a good example of agenda setting in the Gospel of Mark. He gathers his disciples, mostly fishermen. These he has chosen to be his students (the word *disciple*), then also his colleagues ("I do not call you servants any longer, . . . I have called you friends" [John 15:15]), and, after his death, they will serve as his primary witnesses (the word *apostle*). Before they start out in their work together, it will be necessary for them to know what they are expected to be doing. You can imagine how difficult it would have been for Jesus to present some kind of job description for what the disciples were getting into! Yet, he announces a clear goal. Until now they have been fishers for fish. Now, he is going to teach them to be fishers of people (Matt 4:19, Mark 1:17).

Had the leader been anyone other than Jesus, the goals may have appropriately been set by the team, group, or committee, together with the leader. Still, there is something to be learned here. The goal of being "fishers of people" is open enough to allow for creativity of the individual members of the group and allows for a variety of ways to accomplish the goal. Yet it is also clear enough to constitute an announcement of the main purpose of their shared mission on the part of their leader, Jesus.

Good Leaders

- set goals for (or with) the individual, team, group, or committee;
- make sure the goals are doable and open to encourage creativity.

MAKE PRAISE SHORT AND HONEST (LUKE 8:42–48): JESUS PRAISES A WOMAN'S TRUST

The offering of praise is a vital part of any kind of leadership of people. Still, if the leader continually gives praise or heaps on praise inappropriately, too much, or too often, then the recipients may have negative reactions. They might, for example, cease to believe that the praise is deserved. On the other hand, they may come to expect it and never learn to praise themselves adequately, expecting too much of it from the leader.

In a moving narrative in the Gospel of Luke, the crowd is pressing in on Jesus. One desperate woman who has been hemorrhaging for twelve years comes up behind him and, in the hopes of being healed, touches the hem of his clothes. He senses her silent presence and asks, "Who touched me?" (verse 45). The woman is terrified and trembling but finally admits that she was the one and also that she has been healed. Jesus' praise of her action is immediate, short, and honest. He says to her, "Daughter, your faith has made you well, go in peace" (verse 48). This is a simple healing story, but it contains a good example of Jesus' willingness to offer short, clear, and honest praise. This woman must have been at her wits end because the story relates that the doctors had not been able to cure her even though she had spent all her money on them. This woman must also have been afraid. Her condition of bleeding all those years had also made her ritually unclean by the standards of her religion and therefore unwelcome in the sanctuary for worship all this time. So, in many ways, she had been left out of the community. Still, she had built up the courage to come up behind

Jesus, work her way through that crowd, and touch his garments, believing that this touch alone would be enough to cure her.

His words to her are so beautiful and also practical. As short as it is, his response is praise in three parts. First of all, he calls her "daughter," a beautiful family word to use to this complete stranger! That alone must have been soothing and healing to her ears. Second, he gives her personally all the credit for the healing when he says, "Your faith has made you well." Third, there is a sending. "Go in peace," Jesus says to her. There is much implied here. Included in this very short message of praise is "Do not be afraid anymore," suggesting, "May your life be peaceful after all the turmoil you have suffered" and "Everything will be OK. This is the beginning of your new life." His praise of her has been very short, but the woman has been empowered.

So, we see as leaders how powerful a simple, short but deserved praising can be!

Good Leaders

- understand the vital importance of praise for those who follow them;
- make the praise honest and succinct;
- know that either too few sincere praises or too many (undue) praises can be detrimental.

GET PRIORITIES STRAIGHT (MARK 7:14-23): JESUS SAYS, "WATCH YOUR MOUTH!"

When people have chosen to look to you for leadership, they are usually interested and willing to listen to what you have to say. One of the most important aspects of courageous leadership is to know what to say in a variety of situations, to clearly say what you mean, and to know how to say it best. It's just as important to know when not to speak. We, as leaders, continuously must decide when and in what way to speak. We must watch what comes out of our mouths! Because we lead, we will be held responsible. In our modern health-conscious and diet-conscious atmosphere, many of us try to be careful what goes into our mouths. But are we as careful about what comes out of our mouths?

Jesus couldn't have dealt with a more contemporary issue when he talked about this! His disciples were being accused of breaking the Jewish dietary regulations. Jesus points out to those criticizing them that "there is nothing outside a person that by going in can defile" (verse 15). He then goes on to list the kinds of sins that manifest themselves in the form of words that come out of our mouths. "And he said, 'It is what comes out of a person that defiles. For it is from within, from the human heart, that evil intentions come: sexual immorality, theft, murder, adultery, avarice, wickedness, deceit, debauchery, envy, slander, pride, folly. All these evil things come from within, and they defile a person'" (verses 20–23).

Do we spend more time worrying about our calorie or carbohydrate count than on what we choose to say? Most of us don't think of ourselves as practitioners of envy, slander, pride, folly, or any of the rest of the evils on Jesus' list. Yet, when we take another look, we see that he wasn't talking about evil actions; he was referring to (and I quote) "evil intentions." We may be innocent of acting in these ways, but, on the other hand, it is possible that some of us have a way to go before we're clear of any thoughts or intentions related to the items on that nasty list. Instead of feeling self-righteous because we've followed the rules, as leaders, we need to also guard our thoughts and intentions and, along with these, also the words that come out of our mouths. It's not an easy task but well worth the effort!

Good Leaders

- regularly monitor and evaluate their thoughts and intentions as well as actions;
- never speak in ways that demean others or themselves;

- choose to speak in a straightforward, clear, and sincere way.

VALUE HONEST DIALOGUE (JOHN 4:5–30): A WOMAN AT THE WELL

Now, we've considered the importance of the words that come out of our mouths. Still, we may think that, as leaders, we're required to use a certain amount of guile to get our point across or get the job done. The fact is, however, that directness and honesty are prerequisites for good relationships.

The truth is hard to come by. People really appreciate a person who speaks in a forthright manner. The Gospels offer a particularly good example of this kind of honest dialogue, one between Jesus and a woman he meets at a well near the Samaritan city known as Sychar. The woman is a stranger and a Samaritan (not a Jew like Jesus). The two find themselves alone together at this well. She has come alone to get water, and the disciples have left Jesus and gone to look for food. Jesus chooses to start up a conversation with this woman, even though it is not customary or even appropriate for a Jewish man to talk with an unaccompanied woman, especially one he doesn't know. Their conversation is particularly honest and forthright. Jesus starts out with a simple request: "Give me a drink." She responds with a question: "How is it that you, a Jew, ask a drink of me, a woman of Samaria?" (verse 9). The repartee has begun! Jews and Samaritans did not share things in common, as the text goes on to tell us. (In fact, Jews and Samaritans did come out of a shared religious heritage, and as we know, it is often true that the closer people are, the more animosity they tend to be capable of exhibiting toward each other.) Jesus responds to her by saying that if she knew who he was, she'd be asking him, and he'd be giving her living water. The woman's retort seems curt but very bright. We suspect she is being sarcastic, but we can't be sure, when she says, "Sir, give me this water so that I will never be thirsty or have to keep coming here to draw water" (verse 15). The conversation moves the possible sarcasm up a notch when Jesus suggests she should go, call her husband, and come back. The woman admits that she, indeed, has no husband. "You are right," says Jesus, pointing out that she's had five men who were not her husband! The woman continues in what appears to be a sarcastic manner again, saying, "Sir, I see that you are a prophet!" (verse 19). Now, it seems she may be pushing Jesus into a theological discussion centered on the well to which they have both come for water. Her people, she points out, have always worshiped at the mountain, but the Jews now say Jerusalem is the only place to worship. We might expect Jesus to respond that his people are right and her ancestors wrong. Surprisingly, his answer is this: "But the hour is coming and is now here when the true worshipers will worship the Father in spirit and in truth, for the Father seeks such as these to worship him. God is spirit, and those who worship him must worship in spirit and in truth" (verses 23–24). She says she does understand that the Messiah is coming, and Jesus tells her that this Messiah is "the one who is speaking to you" (verse 26). Surprisingly, we do not get a direct response to this from the woman. Instead, the disciples return, and she goes on her way. We are told only that she tells others that this man she has met may well be the Messiah they've all been waiting for.

This text from the Gospel of John, possibly written as late as the year 95–110 CE, clearly demonstrates the theological agenda of the Gospel writer—that is, that Jesus is the Messiah. At the same time, it has also offered us an example of a most exciting, honest conversation. The openness of the words of Jesus and the woman to each other, including her willingness to respond to him so forthrightly and brightly, show us how speedily the important part of an agenda can come to the fore when a conversation's participants are truly willing to engage in honest dialogue.

In this chance conversation between two strangers, it appears that everybody wins. We can assume, although it does not actually say so, that Jesus did get a cup of cool water from the woman to quench his thirst. We can also see that the woman was willing to prod him more and more deeply into conversation while allowing herself to be more and more open about what was on her mind.

Jesus, clearly, gave her much food for thought because, on leaving the place, we are told she was anxious to go out and spread the news of her encounter with him.

Good Leaders

- know that open and honest discourse can lead to good results;
- understand that directness and sincerity are the prerequisites of good relationships;
- realize that communication with those who are different can be fruitful for both.

DON'T CHEAT (MATT 5:27–30): STRAIGHT TALK FROM JESUS

There's surely no leader who is without temptations of one sort or another. The more successful the leader, the more temptations are likely to arise. There's more than one way a person can cheat. People often long for things that don't belong to them and, sometimes, even for relationships that are inappropriate. Those who lead others are required to live with integrity. Not just in their actions, but even what they and others are thinking can often profoundly affect outcomes, relationships, and the work they are doing.

We all know we should not "cheat in our heart," but we may forget that this is about more than adultery. It is also about loyalty and integrity. This passage from the Gospel of Matthew about adultery is being used here because it offers a clear example. "You shall not commit adultery" is, of course, one of the Ten Commandments (Exod 20:14, Deut 5:18). But Jesus moves the issue forward another step. He says, "You have heard that it was said, 'You shall not commit adultery.' But I say to you that everyone who looks at a woman with lust has already committed adultery with her in his heart" (Matt 5:27–28). (This is a classic Jewish [Old Testament] argument known as "from the lesser to the greater," where the teacher forwards the argument by taking the issue one step further. "You have heard . . . but, I tell you . . ." This shows that Jesus was a rabbi skilled in the Jewish rhetorical styles of his day.)

As if we didn't have enough rules to follow! Now after convincing ourselves that Jesus is more interested in the heart of law than the rule of law, we have a lesson that seems to require both the letter of the law and the heart of it. The point, however, is simple, vital to human relationships, and not just about sexual or marital behavior. Jesus is pointing out that, in all our relationships, it's not only the act that counts but also the intention behind the act, the heart of it.

Loyalty, which is at the core of any relationship, is destroyed when any kind of cheating (internal or external) takes place, simply because to cheat is to lie. The lie is the betrayal that happens long before any act itself takes place. And lying can be every bit as devastating for the liar as it is for the person or persons who are lied to.

All good relationships are built on loyalty. One Hebrew word for love is *hesed*. This word describes the biblical kind of love, such as God's love for humankind. Although the word encompasses a variety of the meanings for love in English, its meaning includes "loyalty." Without real loyalty there can be no real love. To be longing for what doesn't belong to us is, of course, selfish. It is also inconsiderate of all parties, especially of ourselves.

Good Leaders

- know that, in many respects, the intention is as important as the act;
- realize that loyalty includes what goes on in the mind and not just the actions.

NOURISH THEM (JOHN 6:1–14): FEEDING THE CROWDS

Most employees, team members, or followers want to be appreciated for the work they do, and all people desire work that has a worthy purpose. It has been shown repeatedly that having meaningful work and being appreciated are more important to most people than even salaries or promotions.

One excellent way to communicate with employees, business colleagues, or committee members you lead is to simply share a meal. It is often the experience of sharing potluck dinners that brings people to clubs or to church and also keeps them coming back, not because of the food itself but because of the genuine satisfaction of eating and drinking in fellowship. This appears to have been true even in the very early church. A shared meal is about much more than eating. It can be about a different kind of nourishment, the joy of sharing. A meal taken together, however simple, can have profound implications as an unspoken symbol of mutual acceptance and trust. Shared meals have a way of bonding people.

The Bible offers a story in which Jesus was followed by a large crowd of people anxious to hear him speak and hoping to be healed. They had gathered at a remote place. After a time, naturally, they started to get hungry. Jesus' response as their leader was to instruct the disciples to feed the people, but neither the disciples nor the people appeared to have brought along any food! Finally, they located a few loaves and fish. The story tells us that when these were prayed over by Jesus and distributed to the gathered crowd, there was found to be enough to nourish them all—the thousands—and there were even leftovers.

All of us need food to nourish our bodies, but the feeding stories about Jesus also bring forward the issue of spiritual hunger. Jesus' promise here is that those who seek and find him are not going to go away hungry. It is particularly interesting in relation to leadership matters to see here that Jesus did not go out looking for these people. Rather, they had come looking for him and were willing to go out to a deserted place just to hear him speak, even perhaps forgetting that they would be needing lunch. In order to be spiritually fed, we can't expect to sit back and wait for everything to come to us. We have to make the effort, and it probably helps, too, if we arrive with an expectation that we're going to learn and grow.

In this feeding story, we also begin to realize that the disciples don't really understand what is going on. Jesus admonishes them when, soon after the feeding, they are already asking him how he intends to feed the next crowd. This suggests that it may be those closest to a given situation who are the very ones not getting the point. It is possible we can get so busy with our project that we miss the main point of what's going on! How could the disciples, of all people, have missed the point? Did they take Jesus for granted? Maybe! We can learn from their mistakes. The best solution to not missing the great things is to practice really being "in the moment." Leaders must stay aware that they might be getting too close to the light and unable to see what is happening.

Another lesson here, especially good for leaders, is simply to trust that our needs will be provided. It is most interesting that the loaves and fish did not materialize from nothing. This "miracle" was not just some kind of magic. They didn't come out of the air. The feeding of the thousands was the result, first, of the generosity of one young boy who offered five loaves and two fish. Only then was the multiplication possible, coming from what started as a small and very human gift freely given. One person in a contemporary situation can do the same. The person may give from his or her wealth or out of poverty. The person gives freely, and the gift is sure to multiply, but it takes the courage of that first person to come forward. Then it needs trust and willingness to share on the part of all before any real abundance can happen.

Good Leaders

- know the importance of sharing a meal for building trusting relationships;
- understand that something as simple as a meal can change the mood of things;

- realize that nourishment can mean much more than food and drink;
- see that when people are aware of each other's needs, then "enough" is manifested;
- are wise enough to "stay in the moment" so they don't miss the best part;
- recognize that big things often come from small beginnings.

RAISE A FUSS WHEN NECESSARY (MARK 11:15-19): THE MONEY CHANGERS

Leaders are generally expected to remain in control and never appear to lose their tempers or even raise their voices. But there are times when it may be necessary to raise not only your voice but also the roof! There are occasions when the message will not be received unless it is strongly delivered! In today's public environment, it's not a good idea to anger anyone, if at all possible. Still, good leaders need to know how and when to turn things up a notch or two when it is important.

This is not a story of "Gentle Jesus, Meek and Mild" (this is the title of a popular hymn, words by Charles Wesley [b. 1792] and music by Martin Shaw [b. 1915]). The story of Jesus' purging the money changers from the temple is one of the more dramatic narratives in the Bible. He comes into the temple and overturns the tables of the money changers and the seats of the dove sellers. In addition, we're told that he would not allow anyone to carry anything through the temple. This kind of behavior certainly would have caused quite a stir in Jesus' day! They'd be asking, just as they might today, "Who put you in charge?" What right did this Jesus have to disrupt their day-to-day business, even if it was taking place at the temple? Jesus knew that what he had to teach here was profound. In this instance, making a scene would be the message. God's house, as he said to them, is a house of prayer for all people, and they had, indeed, turned it into a den of robbers! (This same story, when we find it in the Gospel of John [2:13–16], describes his dramatic behavior even more strongly, adding that Jesus made "a whip of cords" and drove the money changers out of the temple, pouring out the coins and overturning the tables.)

As leaders, it's important that we be aware as to whether any anger we might have is being properly directed. We need to let go of, or at least set aside, any anger that we carry internally which could cause confusion between our own personal issues and the matters for which we're fighting. What is righteous anger? It's nearly always anger about the suffering of others or against those who are able to stop people's pain but unwilling to do so.

The timing of outrage is also important, although that is not always easy to handle. You don't want to be out of control. Will your behavior be misunderstood? Will it appear to be misdirected? It's not, of course, that we can actually "stage" our anger, but we need to be able to use it when it is most needed and try to contain it when it might be inappropriate.

As leaders, we'll nearly always behave quietly and calmly. In general, we'll have much better success that way. Still, there will be times when that commonly good behavior just won't be enough to get a vital message across. It's good to ask yourself well in advance just if, and when, you might be willing to make a scene or cause a disturbance. When will it be right to fight (verbally, at least) for what is right? It helps us as leaders to know, as Jesus showed, that there is a time even for this kind of behavior! When you know for sure that you're right, but when you also know it counts for others, and when you're sure there is no other way to get their attention, then find the courage to raise a fuss and the grace to do so in an appropriate manner.

Good Leaders

- remain calm in nearly all situations;
- are willing and ready to raise a fuss when necessary.

SPEAK (OR DON'T SPEAK) TO POWER (MARK 15:1-5, JOHN 18:33-38): JESUS AND PILATE

As a leader, you know you're constantly making decisions about what to say, when to speak, and sometimes whether to speak at all. Although we don't always think in these terms, such decisions are often related to who holds the most power.

Jesus is brought before Pilate. Pilate, clearly, holds the worldly power in this situation. Like the power of many today, Pilate's power is not as an independent. He represents Rome and Caesar. He is working as a high government official in this particular place. Pilate is a political leader.

If we were reading about the encounter of Jesus and Pilate for the first time, we might guess that its literary purpose was to provide a scene for a showdown between the two. To our surprise, we would realize that, in the version from the Gospel of Mark, Jesus is practically silent. The few words he does speak do not move any argument forward. When Pilate says, "Are you the King of the Jews?" Jesus answers only, "You say so" (Mark 15:2). Jesus has been accused of many things by the chief priests, and Pilate asks him if he has no answer. It is said, "But Jesus made no further reply, so that Pilate was amazed" (Mark 15:5).

There is definitely a time when it is appropriate and the best decision on your part to say nothing, or as little as possible. After all, what's the point of attempting to defend ourselves when we're up against someone much more powerful? They've often already made up their minds before things get to the point of discussion, as with Jesus in this case. Jesus' role modeling here is profound and useful for leadership. We might also note that it does say Pilate was amazed. In this case, the silence of Jesus sent a much more powerful message than any words would have been able to do.

On the other hand, there are times when it's good to speak your mind, even when those who are listening don't want to hear your message. Strangely, it is the Gospel of John's version of this same story that serves us as an example. Here, Pilate asks Jesus the same question, "Are you the King of the Jews?" (John 18:33).

The writer of this Gospel has Jesus come back with a strong reply, in fact a question: "Do you ask this on your own, or did others tell you about me?" (verse 34). Jesus still didn't directly answer the question, but he has Pilate on the run! Pilate, himself very likely an expert at argument, comes back to Jesus with these words: "I am not a Jew, am I? Your own nation and the chief priests have handed you over to me. What have you done?" (verse 35). Again, in this version of the story from John, Jesus responds without giving Pilate a direct answer. He tells Pilate his kingdom is not of this world. "So you are a king?" says Pilate, goading him (verse 37). Jesus responds that now Pilate himself has said it. Jesus goes on to say he's here to testify to truth. Pilate asks him then, "What is truth?" Pilate, seeming to have won the argument by having the last word, in fact did not win it at all. He tells the leaders, "I find no case against him," (verse 38) and attempts to get Jesus released.

Yes, there are times when, as leaders, we're not only required to speak but really need to have our wits about us to make our words worthy. This often takes hard work. It's not that we can prepare exactly what we will say. But when these kinds of discussions or even arguments come up, we will need to give them a lot of thought in advance. What will we want those in power to know about us or our projects or goals? What do we expect them to do in response to what we will say? Might we be able to convince them to be on our side? Do we want them to be on our side? It's important, if we choose to respond to those more powerful and make our case, that we stay in control of ourselves and do not allow their power to overwhelm us.

Good Leaders

- know that it's sometimes best to say nothing;
- have a good idea when to speak and when to stay silent;
- know there may be more than one way to get what's needed;
- stand up to power with honesty;

- take responsibility for what they choose to say;
- know that, just because they don't win, it doesn't mean they lose!

REFRAME THE STORY WHEN NEEDED (MARK 14:3-9): A WOMAN ANOINTS JESUS

On many occasions in leadership, we have the choice of taking something that is said or done either in one way (a good way) or another (not so good). Often, the most obvious reaction to a person's words or actions is that we're offended, or we assume the person had a negative intention. A second choice for us is to look for the good in what's been said or done, if at all possible.

Shortly before his arrest, Jesus found the good in a situation that certain others perceived as only negative. His time on this earth was ending. He was invited to a dinner party. At the gathering, a woman approached him, carrying an alabaster jar of costly oil. She broke open the jar and anointed Jesus' head. Some of the people at the gathering remarked that what the woman had done was irresponsible and wasteful because that jar of oil could have been sold and could have gone a long way to help the poor! They even scolded the woman for her act. It is certainly true, as it always has been, that there are needy people who should be helped. Jesus always had a great concern for the poor. Still, in this case, he has chosen to look only at the positive side of the woman's action toward him and see it only as a gift of loving generosity. He has reframed what could have been viewed as a negative event by proclaiming to all present that this woman has done this as an act of kindness, in order to anoint him in advance for his burial. The pouring of the oil had already taken place and nothing could undo it. Some saw only what was wrong in what the woman had done. Jesus chose to see only what was right!

You, as a leader, will have many chances to choose how you will interpret events in your leadership life. Look for the good and spread the good news about it when you can.

Good Leaders

- assume that what others are doing is for good purposes, unless they know otherwise;
- if they have a choice, take things as having a positive motivation.

SPEAK PLAINLY (MATT 5:33-37): JUST SAY YES OR NO

We've all heard the old adage that if the used car salesman smiles and says, "Trust me," then you'd better not buy the car! We know it's not generally a good idea to speak too much about how honest we are. It should simply be that our word is our bond. We do what we say we are going to do if at all possible, and if we say we will not do a thing, then that is the end of it. This way, people know they can trust us and, over time, will not likely question our integrity. Now of course, there will be times when, for any number of reasons, we're simply unable to do what we said we would. Still, if our reputation is one of integrity, it is likely to be understood and accepted.

The concept of speaking plainly may seem old-fashioned, but leaders of quality will recognize that it is still important today. Now, there are any number of written and signed agreements and contracts that legally bind us to the promises we have made verbally. Still, as in ancient times, these same promises are often broken, either due to circumstances or deliberately. It may be impossible not to be charged with breaking promises, considering the litigious environment in which most of us exist. Still, the best we can do is to intend to be true to our word and then try our best to follow through.

The Bible has warned us not to swear (or make promises, in this case) falsely. Jesus again employs a classic rabbinic type argument, that of taking an issue and moving it one step further, when he says, "Do not swear at all. . . . Let your word be 'Yes, Yes' or

'No, No'" (verses 34, 37). Extraneous promises do not add to the importance of these simple words.

Good Leaders

- say what they mean and mean what they say;
- try not to make promises they can't keep;
- stick to their plans if at all possible.

LEAVE ROOM FOR INTERPRETATION AND CREATIVITY (MARK 10:17–27): JESUS GIVES A HINT

One mistake that too many leaders make is to do too much of the work and the thinking by themselves, without any input from others, and also to come to too many conclusions before a process has taken place. When they do this, they miss the chance to take advantage of the creative power of their people. The people are given the answers in final form, like a beautiful package tied up with ribbon. It may look very pretty, but the trouble is that nobody ever finds out how the results might have looked if everyone participated.

Jesus spoke to the people in parables, and he regularly left his words open-ended, so much so that, after over two thousand years, we're still busy coming up with new and powerful interpretations of them. Just one example can be found in the tenth chapter of Mark. Here, a man runs up to Jesus and asks him what he must do to inherit eternal life (verse 17). Jesus gives him a challenging answer, suggesting he sell all he has and give it to the poor. The man is shocked and leaves in silence. Jesus can probably see that this scenario has disturbed his followers because he says to them, "How hard it will be for those who have wealth to enter the kingdom of God!" (verse 23). They're perplexed. He goes on. But instead of explaining exactly, he gives a metaphor, saying, "It is easier for a camel to go through the eye of a needle than for someone who is rich to enter the kingdom of God" (verse 25). They were looking for an answer, an explanation, but instead he has given them something more confusing to think about. They know literally that a camel can't go through the eye of a needle, so they must figure out what on earth he might have meant.

How many interpretations have come for this passage, over the centuries and millennia? Some say the "Eye of the Needle" was the name of the gate going into the city of Jerusalem and that it would indeed be easy for a person to walk through but almost impossible for a burden-loaded camel. Could Jesus have meant that? Or is he actually saying those who are rich have little chance of getting into heaven? Note, however, that he didn't say anything specifically here about "eternal life," which is what the rich man had asked him about. Rather, Jesus used the term "kingdom of God." Did he mean the afterlife or was he talking about their lives right then? The answer, academic or theological, is only that we do not and cannot know what he meant. Jesus was allowing the disciples to think the matter through for themselves. He did not condemn the rich man. And soon, he explained to the disciples, who were getting quite concerned, that "for mortals it is impossible, but not for God; for God all things are possible" (verse 27). Here, as on so many occasions, Jesus opened up a channel for thought instead of choosing to completely wrap up the package. We encounter this type of experience when we listen to musical performances (particularly vocal ones) in which the performer presents ideas but leaves adequate room for listeners to interpret for themselves the full meaning of the lyrics and music. Delightful! This kind of performance leaves the audience with a sense that the performer trusts them to fill in the blanks from their own experiences, giving the music a meaning that is for them alone.

Good Leaders

- present the ideas, the plan, or the challenge but don't wrap everything up in advance. They leave room for "interpretation";
- give their people a chance to breathe and be creative.

Chapter II

Leaders as Their Best Selves

As LEADERS, WE WANT to put our best foot forward at all times. We can learn a lot from Jesus about being our best selves. Let's take a look again at related aspects of his life and leadership.

TAKE ADVICE FROM STRANGERS (MARK 7:24–30): JESUS LEARNS FROM AN OUTSIDER

You may not have really thought about this as a leader, but the outsider is, at times, the best person to size up a situation correctly. The outsider often has good vision because he or she has no agenda. Or the outsider may be the only one who is free to or willing to speak the truth. People on the "inside" of a given situation are sure to have at least some reasons that are one-sided for their opinions. The outsider, on the other hand, comes with a clean slate and often a keen eye. It can be a very good idea not to turn this person away.

It's important for leaders to have a network of friends, good colleagues, and supporters to call on when things get difficult. Still, there are times when we must deal with those who are not the ones we would call "our own." Most difficult are the situations where we have to ask for help from someone who is outside our company, community, or comfort zone. It takes courage to approach such a person, make our needs clearly known, and even be willing to allow them to help us solve our problems.

A stranger, a Syrophoenician woman, approached Jesus and asked him to heal her sick daughter. She came at a bad time because Jesus was tired. He had come to that place to rest a while. He may have been planning to pray and seek answers to questions about the direction of his life and ministry. At first, he rejected the woman. He told her that any nourishing or healing he had to offer was intended to be food for the children (implying the children of Israel), in other words, not for the likes of her—even comparing her people to dogs! Most people, we might guess, would have walked away from such a confrontation. Instead, this outsider woman chose to persist in a way that was powerful and brilliant, responding to Jesus that even the little dogs under the table get the crumbs that people have thrown down. Because Jesus was willing to accept these words of reprimand from a stranger, for that moment their roles were momentarily reversed, and she became the teacher. She taught Jesus that it is always the right time to offer help when the person in need is standing right in front of you! She reminded him that it is not up to those who do the healing to decide one is worthy of God's generous favor and another is not! She reminded Jesus, who had inferred that his call was only to heal his own people, that all people belong to God, and therefore, all people are deserving of a hearing and a healing.

Jesus, as we might expect, healed her daughter. He also served as a teacher to her in this same chance encounter. He showed that stranger, that Syrophoenician woman, that even in her time of deepest need, she could be a conduit of God's message and a facilitator of learning for him as well as for the healing of her daughter. She learned from this encounter with Jesus that others may be able and even willing to help you even though they are not a part of your community or group, but that you need first to have the humility and courage to ask for that help.

Straight talk with strangers is not always pleasant, but leaders need to know that it is very often worth the trouble. We who lead must be willing to open ourselves to communicate with those who are not part of our immediate circle, and we have to be open and willing to learn from them.

Good Leaders

- realize it is often possible to learn through open dialogue with people from outside our group (if Jesus can learn something from a stranger, then so can we);
- know that they often must go out of their comfort zone to get their needs met;
- are even willing, at times, to make a fool of themselves to get what they need;
- know that it is worth it when they're doing something for the right reasons for others who need it.

BELIEVE IN YOUR PROJECT (LUKE 17:5–6): THE MUSTARD SEED

The leader needs to be the one who believes most strongly in the project or the goal. It's important, therefore, that we ask ourselves about our own commitments in this regard. But we must realize too that it takes more than just our own efforts, time, and energy to make things happen. Everyone on our team will have to be committed as well. Still, even more than the others, we as leaders must believe in the project.

Jesus uses the smallest seed, a mustard seed, to teach a lesson in believing in something. Seeds and gardening may be simple, but they do offer a good example of trust. If you've ever tried to grow a garden, or even a small plant in your kitchen window, you are aware that you do your part but also that there's much more to it. You plant the seed, and then nature either helps or gets in the way. If the plant receives enough water and sunshine in the right proportions for that particular plant and if all goes well, in time something wonderful and beautiful eventually appears. It may be a succulent fruit or leafy green vegetable to be eaten with great enjoyment, a tree that gives glorious shade, or a delicate flower that brings beauty to everyone who lays eyes on it. Every growth, including growth in any business project, involves a minimum of the same three steps. These are the planting, the nourishing, and a waiting period. When we plant something, we trust that growth will happen. There must be trust or we would never begin. Every big plan for success starts with that tiny seed which is, of course, the idea. Some seeds are smaller than others, but few are large to begin with, at least compared to what we can reap as a result of the planting. Magnificent plants sometimes come from some of the smallest, seemingly useless, seeds. Good leaders will tell us the same is true of many of their plans and projects.

Jesus explains that a person's faith may start out as miniscule as a mustard seed. Yet with nourishment, patience, and time, faith will grow. As leaders, we must believe in our plan or our project and also have faith in our people and ourselves.

Have faith. Trust in your project! All this is good advice, but the question is how do we get that trust? How can we deal with our doubts about our plan? A great example is that of the would-be singer who goes to a voice teacher for lessons and every week the teacher says the same thing. "Sing beautifully. That will be fifty dollars, please." A lot of good those lessons will do! Everyone wants to sing beautifully, but they go to the teacher to find out *how* to do it! So, how does a leader get the trust needed to believe in the success of the project?

First, it's good to be aware that doubt is closely connected with faith. A person might declare he or she has no doubts at all, but it's usually more honest to admit and face any doubts so we can move forward in sincerity. The famous metaphysical poet John Donne is believed to have said that in order to know the truth, one should start with one's doubt about it. It's the doubt that gets us asking questions about our project. Doubt may be the very mustard seed that starts trust growing. It's perfectly normal to question our ideas before we settle on plans for fulfilling them, and we need to remain open to any new ideas that those doubts might bring. As long as we have doubts and questions, we stay open to a wealth of new possibilities as to how our project can proceed to success.

It is also a fact that believing is a gift. Having strong faith in our project is something that might not come to every leader with equal ease. Some people are just doubters by nature while others tend to jump in and say yes to things rather quickly. So if believing is a gift, then how do we get some? We can't really talk ourselves into it. Neither can we intellectualize ourselves into being "believers" in our project.

In the case of the gift of religious faith, one of the important ways to get it is to put oneself in the presence of people who already believe. People of faith have a way about them that helps others find faith. This is surely true as well of any project of which we are leader. We need to surround ourselves with people who believe in the project. If the project is valid, it likely will not be long until we have put away any doubts.

The next things that are needed to grow our belief in the project are the nurturing and the nourishing. These will make belief grow from that small mustard seed into something powerful and life-changing. We participate to help make it happen and to watch in amazement.

Our belief in the importance of our project will also grow if it is related to helping others or to building up a better community or world. Giving in some way to those outside our immediate family and community, and putting our money where our mouth is, are the core parts of the identity of someone who believes. Because we are aware that the world and life itself are gifts that we did not earn, we are called to share our resources so that success we have is for everyone and not just ourselves. Any success that is just for us can prove to be less than satisfying. A hope or a plan for success shared with others is sure to increase our belief in our project or plan.

Good Leaders

- know that they need to plant, nourish, and be patient;
- know that the smallest amount of belief or trust can grow and flourish;
- understand that when we really believe in something, we can "move mountains."

LOOK THEM STRAIGHT IN THE EYE (LUKE 13:10–17): A BENT WOMAN

It's easy to tell a person to look life straight in the eye, but it is not always so easy to do it. Far too many leaders engage in what we might call defensive behavior, playing it safe and being unwilling to take chances. Too many people are overly careful about human interaction, avoiding every chance of getting to know new people and behaving with caution even among those they say they count as their friends. When we do this, it indicates an unspoken lack of trust in ourselves, in others, or both. For leaders to be successful, it is necessary to stop hiding fears and feelings, stop playing it safe, and to be fully honest with our people.

Jesus meets up with a bent-over woman in what, at first, looks like yet another healing story. The story's main purpose may well be importantly to demonstrate that Jesus is God's chosen one, but the narrative offers a secondary and perhaps more immediate lesson for leaders. To find it, however, let's look away from the person of Jesus for a minute or two and focus on the woman he is healing. Observe her behavior before and after the healing occurs.

If we study the Greek of this text, there are some things to be discovered that may easily be missed if just read in English translation. Luke 13:11 says, "And just then there appeared a woman with a spirit that had crippled her for eighteen years. She was bent over and was quite unable to stand up straight." First, this woman is said to have had a spirit of something—and whatever it is, she's had it for a long time, eighteen years! Only after that has been said do we learn that she is bent over. So, we don't know if the writer is trying to tell us this woman is bent double by disease or if she is bent double by dis-ease (lack of ease)! Other translations say she had a spirit of infirmity (NKJV). It may only mean she had osteoporosis and was not physically able to straighten up her body. Or maybe not! Either way, how hard is it for any of us when we have an attitude or a "spirit of weakness"? Did this woman possibly have an attitude of sickliness because of something that had happened to her somewhere over the course of her life? Was she afraid of something? Lots of people can't see straight ahead because of fear. Had life frightened her off from looking the world in the eye? We can't know for sure whether she had a physical ailment, and we don't know from the translation whether she was completely bent over, only partially unable to stand upright, or emotionally held down. As the story continues, Jesus lays hands on her and we are told that "immediately she straightened up and praised God" (verse 13). In other words, she was set upright or possibly set straight.

What the woman does next is quite amazing. She doesn't get down on her knees and thank Jesus. She doesn't even seem to be surprised. The story tells us the woman begins immediately to praise and glorify God. That spirit of weakness she suffered had very likely not stopped her from coming to the synagogue up to that time, even though it must have slowed her down. She was able to attend and be present with the others, but she had not been able, it seems, to fully participate until she could get rid of that so-called "spirit of infirmity." Jesus freed her from her suffering, and immediately she was on her way, restored to wholeness. Now the woman was capable of openly and fully praising God. And that is exactly what she chose to do.

When the leaders of that synagogue complained because Jesus had healed the woman on the Sabbath (a day that people were not supposed to work), Jesus was quick to respond. He spoke to them of her, calling her a "daughter of Abraham" (verse 16), to remind them that she was one of their own people: a Jew, and therefore offered the fullness of life by God. Jesus also said she had been "bound by Satan" (verse 16) and that it was Jesus who had set her free. Surely a worthy enterprise for the Sabbath! Today, we don't use the terminology of binding and loosing, or of Satan holding us hostage, and such. Nevertheless, as leaders (and followers) we often do allow ourselves to be held back. We find ourselves bound by doubts and by fears. We may not have physical illnesses, but we leaders often get ourselves "tied up" by insecurities and bent over with worries, no matter how calm things may seem on the outside. When we do this, we find ourselves unable to think clearly or to experience life in its fullness.

Fears can keep leaders and their teams from being whole and from truly living. Seeing or not seeing ourselves as whole is at least a part of what this bent woman biblical story is about. Too often, leaders will keep their budgets too low. Or they may choose to take careful steps toward modest growth instead of courageous steps toward substantial growth. This happens because they're afraid to see themselves as whole, afraid to trust and believe that wonderful things can happen in their companies or communities. What can evolve for us if we burst the bonds of our over-carefulness, put away our fears, and allow the spirit to move us in bigger ways? Jesus, as a great leader, knew what could happen. If we were less fearful, we could let go of our feelings of lack and give out of our own bounty to help others. We could fling open our doors to people who are different from us and who didn't seem to fit into our plans.

That bent-over woman was healed. What does it really mean to be healed? Healing is not always just about physical illnesses. In the Bible, when God called young Jeremiah, for example, he simply could not accept his new leadership role at first. Jeremiah responded to God by saying, "Ah, Lord God! Truly I do not know how to speak, for I am only a boy" (Jer 1:6). God's answer was, in effect, "So what? I'm calling you! Follow me." Physical infirmities aside, age issues aside, financial problems aside, lack of educational qualifications aside, we are still called to wholeness, called to let God make us whole, and then to respond with a life of praise.

What is a life of praise? It doesn't mean we're praying or singing all the time. A life of praise is essentially a life of joy and ongoing thankfulness. An attitude of praise also produces a life of service. A praising person is one who recognizes that he or she can still be whole even if not physically "cured." A person can live in a continuous state of gratefulness for the gift that is human life. Leaders are very different, and more powerful, when they are thankful people.

Let's consider how that woman who met Jesus changed from a bent-over woman into a praising woman. The story says Jesus laid his hands on her. She was touched by him and then things changed for her. Another metaphor, perhaps! Are we as leaders allowing ourselves to be touched by others? Or are we holding back, thinking we need to be totally self-sufficient?

It's strange but true that people sometimes unknowingly want to hold on to their infirmities, be they visible or invisible. These infirmities offer what is known as secondary gain. If we see ourselves as less than capable, then maybe we won't have to work so hard. Perhaps we won't be asked to do so many things. Maybe we'll get some sympathy. We won't have to commit ourselves and our lives totally to the mission. And we'll always have an excuse ready so we can forgive ourselves too quickly for tasks not accomplished. But in doing all this, we may also never learn what it is to be fully alive and to lead from a position of truly being both healed and whole.

Good Leaders

- face their own failings with honesty;
- live life now. Jesus said, "Give us today our daily bread" (Matt 6:11);
- look life straight in the eye;
- may be weak but know they can still be a conduit for good things;
- know they are called to wholeness, not to brokenness.

LIVE IN TRUST (MATT 6:25-33, LUKE 12:22-31): CONSIDER THE LILIES

Who among us has never worried about whether we were going to have enough, enough to clothe and feed ourselves and our families and provide a roof over our heads? Will we have money for the education of our children and for needed vacations? Are our resources sufficient to cover unexpected medical bills? Will there be enough for retirement or a nursing home if we need one later in life? Will inflation eat up what we have saved? Leaders have the additional worry of feeling responsible, at least to some extent, also for the people who follow them. Will there always be enough money to cover the payroll and business costs? Is the church growing fast enough? Is the business going to continue to thrive into the future? It seems like we can never be really sure we'll have enough to make us feel safe or appeased. How can we stop worrying?

There are many among us who don't really have to worry about the necessities of life. The worry factor or stress level for these people, however, is often just as high as it is with those who are without sufficient resources. Some may worry, as a habit derived from memories of earlier, leaner times. Others may transfer old worry habits from problems that have since been resolved to a new set of things to worry about. Will they be able to responsibly manage the resources in their care? Will the good times end? Do they really deserve this comfort they are enjoying now? Do people in their lives really love them for themselves or is it their money they love? And, if this is not enough, there are always the ups and downs of the stock market and concerns as to whether they have wisely invested their resources. It's a fact that even fortunes come and go. Leaders often also have concerns about their popularity and success. After all, hasn't the world taught us well that we need all these things? Although some competition can be good and concern might be practical, these can easily become extremely harmful. Fear of not having enough in the future can indicate a lack of hope for a positive outcome, a lack of faith in one's own abilities, and even a lack of trust in the ultimate provider. Jesus had the courage to address the issue directly.

Jesus had very strong words to say about all this: a good piece of practical advice that can change us and our leadership, if we are willing to accept it. Jesus said,

> Therefore I tell you, do not worry about your life, what you will eat or what you will drink, or about your body, what you will wear. Is not life more than food and the body more than clothing? Look at the birds of the air: they neither sow nor reap nor gather into barns, and yet your heavenly Father feeds them.... And which of you by worrying can add a single hour to your span of life? And why do you worry about clothing? Consider the lilies of the field, how they grow; they neither toil nor spin, yet I tell you, even Solomon in all his glory was not clothed like one of these.... Do not worry.... But seek first the kingdom of God and his righteousness, and all these things will be given to you as well. (Matt 6:25–29, 31, 33)

This is often the place where the experienced, hard-nosed executive says, "That's church talk. It won't work in the real world!" But why do we so often forget that Jesus lived in this very real world and in tremendously difficult times? Jesus didn't say not to concern ourselves about doing a good job. What he said is that worry, in itself, is a total waste of our time! We already know that, of course, but we just don't want to practice it. A good leader really must live in trust and carry on with courage through the inevitable ups and downs. It's difficult to be successful or to lead others if we don't believe things will turn out for the best.

Good Leaders

- trust that their needs will be met but work to make it happen;
- don't waste time worrying;
- work on maintaining a positive attitude;
- keep as priority the good relationships rather than just belongings.

KNOW WHERE YOU FIT (LUKE 14:1, 7-11): YOUR PLACE AT THE TABLE

It is vital, as leaders, that we try to maintain a pretty good sense of where we and our group, organization, or project fit into the larger picture. What that big picture is will vary depending on your situation. It's also vital that however smoothly things may be going along, we do maintain honest humility about where our project properly fits into the bigger picture.

There's a fine story in the Gospel of Luke about Jesus attending a dinner party. At this party, he notices that the guests are choosing places of honor for themselves. He uses this opportunity to say,

> When you are invited by someone to a wedding banquet, do not sit down at the place of honor, in case someone more distinguished than you has been invited by your host, and the host who invited both of you may come and say to you, "Give this person your place," and then in disgrace you would start to take the lowest place. But when you are invited, go and sit down at the lowest place, so that when your host comes, he may say to you, "Friend, move up higher"; then you will be honored in the presence of all who sit at the table with you. For all who exalt themselves will be humbled, and those who humble themselves will be exalted. (Luke 14:8–11)

The story itself, of course, is not about one specific dinner party. Jesus is likely referring to a coming time when all things will be turned upside down. Still, mutual respect and moderate behavior never go out of style. Have you as a leader changed your behavior over the years to fit in with what seems your acceptable position in society? And what rules of etiquette do you maintain, no matter what expectations come and go?

Have you ever attended a wedding banquet and watched to see where the religious leaders chose to sit for the dinner? Did they seem to assume they were an integral part of the wedding party and, as such, make a beeline for the "head table"? Or maybe they hung back close to the rear door in humility, fully expecting to be found worthy and be called or brought forward. Or did they simply enter the banquet room, assuming there would be a place for them somewhere among the gathered community? In recent decades, ministers (who had earlier performed the wedding service at the church) have been called up to sit at the head table less and less. This means that, more often, they end up sitting at the back of the banquet room for the entire evening, all too often seeming just a bit disgruntled.

In this banquet story, Jesus is giving practical advice for everyone but especially for leaders. It's best not to push yourself forward, he says, but be patient and let others indicate whether you are to be honored and chosen for a special place of honor. Honor is always bestowed by others and according to their time schedule, not our own.

This same biblical story also addresses the way we view others in relation to ourselves. If we think we're special it's likely to show because our motivation is different, and therefore our responses are different. It's not just our actions that are in clear view but also our attitudes.

Jesus teaches that we are all God's people, called to live together in harmony. We cannot truly be in harmonious community if we perceive ourselves as superior to others. Jesus' little bit of practical banquet etiquette advice here goes to the core of good business relationships as well as in making a better world. War happens when one nation thinks itself superior. Instead of taking their place at the banquet of life equally along with others, too many head straight for that "head table" place of honor, pushing everyone else to the periphery.

We all know humility is a virtue. Some take it to extremes and, in doing so, are again positioning themselves for being lifted above the crowd. True humility is not about being intentionally lowly. It's more about knowing, or at least having a clue, where we realistically fit in. In any situation there are probably others who can do what we do just as well as or even better than we can. On the other hand, each of us likely has gifts that the others don't possess. It's the combination and the variety of gifts we employ as we work together that makes things better for everyone and better for ourselves.

In many cases, we'll be raised to higher positions as leaders. But, of course, it can never be that we put ourselves there. Honor cannot be chosen by us. As I said earlier, honor is always bestowed by others who have found us worthy and decided we deserve it.

Good Leaders

- try to always be aware of where they fit in the scheme of things;
- maintain their humility throughout their success;
- stay open to new ideas.

BE ACCOUNTABLE (MARK 10:35-45): TWO BROTHERS ASK FOR FAVORS

How much energy do you as a leader put into recreating yourself? We want a promotion at work. We seek out a life partner whom we feel is up to our ideals. We long for and work toward making friends in higher places. We hope for a better standard of living. It is certainly not discouraged in our society to try for success or even reach for the stars. For this reason, we can understand why, in the Gospel of Mark, the brothers James and John decide to ask Jesus for a big favor: they want him to set them up in a special place on either side of him when he comes into his glory. In the Matt 20:20-28 version of the same story, the request is placed in the mouth of the mother of the two disciples. In Mark, it was common for the disciples to make mistakes and to miss the point. But the author of Matthew (a later Gospel) may have considered it inappropriate for disciples to be anything but exemplary in every way. Why not put the request in the mouth of their mother? After all, mothers always want the best for their sons. Who can blame mothers?

The writer's purpose, of course, cannot be known for sure in our times. It may be that such a version of the same story existed in oral form and was simply included here. More likely, however, the narrative from Mark was adjusted in Matthew to keep the disciples from any "bad press" that would come as a result of such a highly inappropriate request. Whatever the reason, the writer of Mark is much more willing than that of Matthew to describe the disciples' human foibles and fallibility. In both Mark and Matthew, Jesus denies the request, telling them that it's not his decision because only God will decide who will sit where when it comes to heaven. He explains, too, that this is something they really have no right to request. Certainly, there are leaders who attempt social climbing, or who do similar things for the wrong reasons. How many times, even while engaged in doing good for others, are leaders' primary concerns still for reasons of their own gain: reputation, respect, or social status?

How disappointed Jesus must have been to hear two of his closest followers and best friends asking to be lifted above the others. Their request gives the impression that, at the very least, these brothers had missed the point of just about everything he's been trying to teach them! The good news is that, following their incredible faux pas in asking this favor, the brothers were allowed to continue as disciples, as if the selfish words had never been spoken. There's nothing that suggests they were reprimanded further. As a leader, Jesus knew human nature and human foibles. He also must have understood that there was no point in saying any more about it.

All who lead others may be tempted to try to raise themselves above their peers on occasion. And they'll probably see those who follow them doing the same. Jesus took the opportunity to turn the disciple brothers' mistake into one of those great teachable moments. Also, he clearly forgave this common human weakness. We can do the same.

It can help if we, as leaders, ask ourselves regularly in what ways we are being tempted to raise ourselves above others. Are we buying into the world's agenda of seeking more and more success, wealth, or popularity at others' expense? Naturally, as a leader you are always going to be in some competition with others who offer the same product, message, or service. Still, it's best to remember that every person offers something unique. For this reason, undue or unfair competition is not in anyone's best interest. If we are leading with integrity, then what we offer will be sufficient. People are never impressed with leaders, companies, or religious institutions that try to be raised up by putting others down.

Good Leaders

- try to ask for the right things and for the right reasons;
- don't engage in unfair tactics to be raised above competitors. They concentrate, rather, on the quality of their own product, message, or service;
- realize they do not know the future. (Even Jesus said he didn't know when the end would come [Matt 24:36], but he kept working for the reign of God.)

LISTEN TO THE POWERLESS (MATT 18:1–6): FROM THE MOUTHS OF BABES

Leaders are required to constantly deal with issues related to power and to be aware of who holds the power at any given time. What happens when that power shifts? Is it always the powerful people who have the answers, or is it sometimes those with less power? When leaders make decisions, are these only in the best interest of the powerful? How will their decisions affect those in weaker positions? And finally and most importantly, what might the vulnerable and powerless among us have to teach those of us who lead?

Jesus presents little children as an excellent example of powerlessness. He not only approves of children but is even willing to set them up as role models for the rest of us. Adults are admonished by Jesus to be like children. He even says that to enter the kingdom of heaven, we must become like little children. In addition, he adds that we would be better to have a millstone around our neck and be thrown into the sea than to harm one of these little ones (Matt 18:6). (This idea about children's worth would likely have seemed quite shocking in Jesus' day. It is generally agreed upon by scholars that in the first century, children were largely seen as being of little value. Small children were unable to carry a load of daily work and unlikely able to contribute in any meaningful way to the current family income. Girls were seen to be of even less value than boys. Because of the patriarchal system, it was the boys who carried on the family name and were likely to be physically stronger and more able to work at a younger age. Children were in many ways a burden until they could work to help the family, then get married, raise their own children, and eventually care for aging parents. This does not mean their existence was not valued in other ways. A woman unable to give birth to a child for whatever reason was looked upon askance in that society. Children were needed for the continuation and increase of the race and family. Still, the individual child in Jesus' time was not given the deference and the attention that so many of today's children receive in our society.)

Jesus was able to recognize the great worth of children. He knew that children possess many attributes. In general, they tend to be more trusting than adults. Children are often quick to forgive and get on with the business at hand. Children stay open to possibilities. Children are generally full of hope. They tend to be continually amazed at just about everything in God's creation. Leaders need to think about how many of these attributes they have lost in growing up and how many more of these childlike qualities they've been shedding as they grow older and supposedly wiser.

Children are vulnerable. They have no choice but to be dependent. Jesus points out, as he lifts up a child in the midst of the gathered community, that all of us are vulnerable. We are totally dependent on God's grace and, in fact, also dependent to a large extent on each other. Our self-sufficiency is most often a myth, as much as we would like to believe in our complete independence.

In lifting up the child, Jesus also reminds us as leaders that the lowly among us have mighty worth, a value that often goes unrecognized. Any family that has a member who suffers from disabilities probably understands this concept and can quickly tell of the worth of those among us who may be the most vulnerable.

They assure us that the presence of these "little ones" brings them gifts and treasures which nobody outside that family could ever begin to understand.

What is the true value of those who are, today, considered the lowest in our society? What would society look like without them? Recent technological advances have forced us to think about a world in the not-so-distant future in which genetic choices could be made in advance of birth to eliminate those who would have been born with mental and physical diseases and disabilities. Can we picture such a world? Are there advantages? And what would we also lose?

The poor are also looked down upon by society. Many are financially vulnerable in our times. Mistakes or selfishness on the part of the wealthy have often caused the poor to be put into these positions. Yet it's the poor who seem also to get blamed for their difficult situation. They're often viewed as stupid, lazy, or weak. Yet somehow the poor survive. Leaders need to recognize that these same people often possess wisdom and spiritual resources to share, of which we know very little. The poor have much to teach us.

The "little ones," the young and the vulnerable, and those without power are continually lifted up by Jesus, who says, "Blessed are the poor in spirit for theirs is the kingdom of heaven" (Matt 5:3). Jesus models his great leadership skill when he reminds us again that we may be looking for our role models in all the wrong places.

Good Leaders

- know there's much to learn from those whom the world despises. Listen to them;
- know that what seems so important to the world isn't always what's important;
- are aware of the effect their work and leadership are having on the most vulnerable;
- are not afraid to ask the vulnerable what they think.

BE WILLING TO DIG IN (JOHN 13:1-9): FEET ARE WASHED

It is sometimes a hard lesson, but it is best if leaders can do (and are also willing to do) whatever they expect their followers to do. A classic example is that of the restaurateur who puts all his or her energies into the business but can't cook. Needless to say, if the cook decides to leave, that can be dangerous!

Jesus was sharing the Passover meal with his disciples, the last meal they would eat together before his death. We are told that he "tied a towel around himself. Then he poured water into a basin and began washing the disciples' feet and to wipe them with the towel" (verses 4b–5). This was normally the work of a servant and certainly not expected of the master. Peter, his beloved disciple, questioned him in performing this lowly act. Jesus' response was that if Peter would not allow him to wash his feet, then "you will have no share with me." Peter then allowed Jesus to wash his feet. Jesus teaches them, "So if I, your Lord and Teacher, have washed your feet, you also ought to wash one another's feet." Jesus has thereby demonstrated to his closest followers the importance of humility in those who lead, but also the fact that you really should not ask people to do something you yourself are not willing to do.

It is best, as a leader, if you know every aspect of the work you expect your followers to engage in. Now, in many cases of course, it's not possible for you to have the same skills that certain of your workers or followers have. Still, you must be willing to dig in and demonstrate to them that you are willing to get your hands dirty. It will show that you respect them and will also show them the importance of humility and a willingness to dig in on the part of the whole team or group.

Good Leaders

- make sure that they know, as much as possible, how to do all aspects of what they expect others to do;

- encourage others to be able to do everything that they do and more! No one should be indispensable and that includes the leader!

LISTEN TO YOUR BOSS (LUKE 22:39-42): NOT MY WILL BUT YOURS BE DONE

This book is for those who lead. Still, most of us who are leaders also have some kind of a boss, or at least we are accountable to someone or some group. It is important that, as we lead others, we don't get such an inflated opinion of ourselves that we forget that person or group. We can assume our bosses know what they're doing and have good judgment, or we wouldn't be working for them. Jesus never forgot to keep in close contact with his boss, God, whom he also called Father or sometimes even Abba, which means more like "Daddy." (We shall not get tied up in deep theological discussions here about Trinitarian relationships, as this is not any kind of theological treatise. Still, even seeing Jesus as an aspect of God in the Trinity implies the importance of relationship.) In the Gospel of John, Jesus is constantly talking about the importance of his close connection to God. When he finds out he is facing death, he prays to God in the garden. He asks God to take this cup from him if it is possible, thus demonstrating his deep and very human suffering. But then, immediately after making the request, he adds these words: "Not my will but yours be done" (verse 42). He has not lived a human life of obedience to God to end it with an act of insubordination.

We don't always know exactly why our bosses want what they want. They are often more deeply involved in the "big picture" than we are and can't always explain why they ask us to do things. It is important that we try to follow their instructions and keep them informed of what we are doing.

Good Leaders

- check in regularly with their bosses;
- listen to their bosses and follow their instructions;
- keep their bosses informed with what they need to know.

DON'T FORGET TO RECHARGE (LUKE 6:12): REST BEFORE DECISION MAKING

One of the biggest mistakes made by both leaders and followers is thinking they can go on without recharging their batteries! Today too many of us have some kind of idea that we're superheroes. Long hours of work without rest will catch up with us for sure. Of course, there are times of emergencies in any company, organization, or group. But we are lying to ourselves if we think we can go on this way for long without rest. Today many people also deal with long commutes in heavy traffic back and forth from their homes, in addition to the hard work they do. The stress can be overwhelming. Our bodies cannot be working continually in emergency mode.

Throughout the Gospels we hear about Jesus taking himself away for a while to pray and to be quiet and alone. If he needed rest, then we certainly do as well. In the Gospel of Luke, Jesus has been arguing with opponents, healing people, and is even finding himself threatened by jealous opponents. Sound stressful? Then the mood changes and the text says, "Now during those days, he went out to the mountain to pray, and he spent the night in prayer to God" (verse 12). This is just one example of Jesus taking himself away from the fray, for time away.

He seems to be refreshed by the time he has spent alone and in prayer because we are told he then is able to go out and choose his twelve disciples. Shortly after this, Jesus is said to be out healing people again and soon offering his magnificent sermon (Luke 6:20–49), which includes the beloved words known as the Beatitudes.

Time alone and time for meditation in whatever form that takes for you as a leader is sure to refresh and renew you and give you some new perspective. When we work nonstop or worry continually, our brain function decreases. Overwork causes fatigue and, in time, can also work away at even the strongest bodies to their detriment. No matter what the demands of our leadership, we simply must find time for rest and renewal.

Good Leaders

- recognize when they are overdoing it;
- make a habit of taking reasonable time for rest and renewal;
- arrange for rest and renewal for those they lead;
- understand that rest time is by no means wasted time.

SHARE CONTROL (MATT 10:1–31): JESUS MAKES THEM FLY

There come times in leadership when it is most important to share power and control and to delegate certain areas of work or authority. Without this, your team or group will never be truly empowered to do their best work. It is all too easy for the leader to keep saying or believing that the people are not ready. If this goes on for too long, it's very likely that you are simply not willing to relinquish control or really trust your people.

Even in the case of Jesus, who clearly was the superior and the authority figure, we can find an excellent example of sharing leadership and control. In the Gospel of Matthew, chapter 10, Jesus summons his disciples and gives them "authority" to do the things that, up to this point, only he himself has been doing (such as casting out unclean spirits and curing diseases and every sickness). But he did not send them without instructions. Interestingly, he told them where not to go, as well as generally what to say and what to do. He also instructed them to go without expectation of payment—that is, for the right reasons. In addition, he wanted them to go without too much equipment, such as extra money, clothes, and baggage. He told them they could expect to be fed and cared for by good people. If there were those who did not treat them well, they were not to stay and contend with these people but, instead, to move on. He warned them that they would be like sheep among wolves and were likely to encounter problems along the way, but they should not be afraid because it would all come out right in the end.

When we relinquish control and send our people out into the world to do what they have learned to do, it might be scary for us. But it's often best for all concerned. We need to be clear with them about what they will and will not need for backup and what problems they might run into. Then, we must trust that they'll follow through and do their best, whatever the circumstances, negative or positive.

Good Leaders

- have the courage to share control and give authority to others;
- make sure the people understand the nature of the mission;
- give clear and simple instructions;
- explain what could go wrong and how they might deal with it;
- encourage those who take on this authority not to be afraid;
- ultimately, trust those to whom they have given the authority.

REMEMBER YOU ARE ALWAYS AN EDUCATOR (LUKE 24:13-35): THE ROAD TO EMMAUS

A leader is always an educator. Those people we work with may be long out of school and may not think of us as teachers, but they will still need our help and direction in order to continue learning and growing.

Throughout his earthly life, Jesus was always teaching, and even the crowds who followed him, in addition to the disciples, understood him to be a teacher (the word *rabbi*, which the people used in referring to Jesus in places like John 1:38, means "teacher"). Two men are heading out toward Emmaus, talking with each other about the things that have recently happened—namely, the crucifixion and death of their beloved leader, Jesus. Suddenly, Jesus himself appears, begins to walk alongside them, and starts asking them questions. Not recognizing him, of course, the men tell him all about how their leader, Jesus, a prophet, was killed and entombed, and then how some women told them that angels had reported he was alive again. They say that some of them had gone out to check but that Jesus had not been seen again. They are sad and disheartened and clearly have no idea who it is they're talking to! Jesus' response is not to say, "Look at me. Don't you recognize me? I'm here! The women were right!" Instead, he carefully and thoughtfully reviews with them how Hebrew Scripture, their own holy books, had told them about what would happen. The text puts it this way: "Then, beginning with Moses, and all the prophets, he interpreted to them the things about himself in all the scriptures" (Luke 24:27). We're not told, even then, that these men figured out who Jesus was. Instead, they invite him to stay for the evening. They share a meal, and he leaves. Later, they finally begin to realize what's happened, saying, "Were not our hearts burning within us while he was talking to us on the road, while he was opening the scriptures to us?" (verse 32). They are excited now and decide that same hour to rush to Jerusalem and tell the rest of the disciples that the Lord is truly risen and had been made known to them in the breaking of the bread (verse 35).

In this narrative, Jesus has chosen to help these men to understand his resurrection, not by the magic of his presence but by the simple, important, and common task of teaching. As he chats with them along the road, he does something very human. He interprets the Scripture and then simply shares a meal with them.

Only later do they realize who it was that was teaching them. After the lessons along the road and then the shared meal, only then are they able to proclaim, "The Lord has risen indeed" (verse 34).

Jesus chose the teaching format throughout his ministry but especially in this wonderful story of the Road to Emmaus. A leader, whatever the format, is primarily a teacher. We can amaze people with our magic-like skills and talents or wow them with our charismatic presence, but in the end, leading others is simply the act of being a good educator and sometimes sharing a meal.

Good Leaders

- take every opportunity to teach those who follow them;
- are willing to repeat lessons when needed;
- understand that the message is more important than their personal charisma.

DON'T GET CAUGHT UP IN YOUR OWN PRESS (LUKE 18:18-19): THEY CALL JESUS GOOD

Leadership, and especially successful leadership, presents a challenge that is seldom spoken about: the challenge of maintaining balance and humility. That is the challenge of those who lead with great acumen and those whose special gifts are recognized by all around them. Everyone has heard one story or another of how some famous person has become caught up in some level of megalomania—that is, they have come to believe their talents give them an unreasonable amount of power over others. Even if they cannot be deemed a megalomaniac, many powerful people get caught up far too deeply in what we might call "believing in their own press." Those who lead must intentionally and carefully maintain their balance. They need to keep a realistic sense of exactly where they fit into the scheme of things.

There is an excellent example of Jesus' behavior in this regard to be found in the Gospel of Matthew. When a ruler comes to him and addresses him as "good teacher" (verse 18) Jesus picks up on the word "good." His quick response is "Why do you call me good? No one is good but God alone" (verse 19). One may wonder why he would say such a thing. We would likely all agree that Jesus was, indeed, a good teacher. But he keeps his focus not on his own goodness but on the goodness of God.

Good Leaders

- maintain a balance between recognizing their own talents and seeing their own flaws and imperfections;
- understand that everything that is said about them (good or bad) is not always true;
- never get caught up in wielding their power unfairly.

Chapter III

Leaders Deal with Change

ALL OF US MUST deal with change. Change is the most consistent fact of life, and one of the most difficult to deal with. Sometimes people in our lives change; sometimes we change! Other times it may be the circumstances that change. We don't really know why matters of change are so hard for most of us, but we can look at how Jesus dealt with issues related to change.

WHEN PEOPLE CHANGE (JOHN 20:10–18): MARY MAGDALENE AT THE GRAVE

When people change, it can be really hard on their friends, family, and colleagues. Still, when they are ready to change, they will, and there is nothing we can do about it except try to adjust. It often doesn't even matter whether their change is for the worse or the better; it still is difficult for others.

There is a great story in the Gospel of John that takes place after the death of Jesus. Mary Magdalene goes to the garden outside the tomb and sees a man there whom she assumes is the gardener. She soon comes to realize that the man she is encountering is, in fact, not the gardener at all but Jesus, her beloved friend. When he calls her by name, she responds immediately with the name by which she has known him, "*Rabbouni*" (verse 17), which means teacher. Jesus seems to have sensed that she would be wanting to cling to him and hold on for dear life because he says to her, "Do not touch me. . . . I am ascending to my father and your father, to my God and to your God" (verse 17).

Surely Mary Magdalene must have longed for Jesus to remain exactly as she had always known him in the world. She would have hoped she could continue sharing the joys and burdens of this life with him, with the disciples, and others. But a great change has come! Now he has been crucified. He has experienced death, and he is forever changed from what he had been in the past. Now Jesus is even more than what he was in life, and he is different. Jesus commands her tenderly, implying that she is not to hold on to the past. She cannot cling to him any longer as the person she has known him to be in the past. This suggests that, if she does try, she will be able to experience him in a new way, now not only as Jesus the man but as Jesus the crucified and risen Christ.

It's important for us as leaders not to cling, protectively, to old ideas and old ways. When something has worked well in the past, it's natural to want to continue with it. But situations change and even people change. We are all different over time. It is often very difficult for those who have known us in the past to accept the fact we have changed. On our part, allowing for others to develop, change, and grow is not always easy but, as leaders, we must do it.

Good Leaders

- know they can't hold on to the past, even if what they did in the past worked well;
- keep eyes open for the best of what has changed and for what is new;

- know they can't control everything. They may be surprised about things they can't control, but they deal with change the best they can;
- try always to deal with change in a positive way by welcoming it.

WHEN THE PLANS CHANGE (MATT 25:1–13): THE BRIDESMAIDS BEFORE THE WEDDING

In leadership, as in life, plans often have to change. Life has a way of surprising us, even when we're planning ahead in the best possible ways. Flexibility is one of the greatest assets a leader can have.

Jesus tells a story of a rather large group of bridesmaids (ten in all) who are waiting for a wedding to take place at an appointed time. Some had made their lamps ready in advance, and these are named as wise. The others are called foolish because they had assumed everything would go exactly as planned and that the bridegroom would arrive at a later time. When it's least expected, there comes an announcement that the bridegroom is already on his way and will soon arrive to lead them to the wedding. The unprepared young women find themselves with no oil for their lamps, so they ask the others, who were prepared, to provide for them from their oil. They refuse and tell the rest to go out and buy their own oil. They go to get oil, but when they return, they find the bridegroom had arrived and everyone has gone on ahead of them to the wedding. The unprepared bridesmaids don't get to be real bridesmaids after all! They thought they could assume the way things would go in the upcoming hours. As a result, they weren't ready for the surprise change in plans and, consequently, missed the entire wedding.

Jesus' message here is a difficult but coldly honest one. Be prepared for surprises, or else! Life can and may very well go on without us if we're not ready at all times for change! Leaders who don't stay watchful for unexpected changes can expect one thing—to lose out. The main purpose of this parable in Scripture has been to talk about being prepared for the end time or afterlife. Still, the point of preparedness can apply just as well to our current lives and daily work in a plain sense. The story shows that in no situation should we become complacent or assume that change will not happen when we least expect it. We can never predict how things will go, what will happen, or when! We have to try our best to be ready for whatever comes. Be alert. Expect change. It's a cliché but it must be said. The fact that change will occur is the only thing in life that can be absolutely guaranteed.

There is another rather pithy wedding story (Matt 22:1–14), which will also be discussed in chapter 8, in which Jesus tells how an inappropriately dressed, last-minute guest is thrown out of a wedding reception. There too, Jesus' message seems particularly strong and demanding. Those who are not watchful and ready can lose out on the celebration. Leaders should never assume things will continue in the status quo. Both life and business often bring surprises that require major and rather speedy changes in plans and direction. And, if we're not ready, we could miss the whole thing!

Often, leaders are distracted from what really counts, getting sidetracked by problems that have little to do with the big picture and finding themselves unready when their real chance comes. We must continuously work to demonstrate a kind of leadership that is centered and focused. People look toward their leaders for these qualities. They want to know that when changes are needed and when the surprises do come (good or bad), those who lead them will be ready to adjust with courage and direction.

Good Leaders

- know life doesn't "happen" on our schedules and that much cannot be planned;
- realize the time for the celebration might be right now;
- focus on what is really important;

- are awake and ready for the coming of good things into their midst;
- don't miss good when it is right in front of them.

WHEN CIRCUMSTANCES CHANGE (LUKE 22:35-38): NEW INSTRUCTIONS

Have you ever been in a situation in which the usual defenses or tactics simply won't work? In general, it's best for leaders to be consistent in their instructions and expectations. This way, people will know what to expect. Changes and surprises can be disconcerting, even disturbing. Still, there are many circumstances that require new instructions and sometimes quick changes in direction. Good leaders must be able to make these changes and get their followers to move with them and not against them. Many people will balk at the very idea of change. Across the board, church members, when facing changes suggested by their pastor, are infamous for their common and classic response, "But, pastor, we've always done it this way before!" This truth finds its way into the business world as well, and even into families, so that change often becomes a bigger problem than it needs to be.

Looking at the life of Jesus, we can see consistency in his advice to his disciples. But there is one occasion where he takes back his words and instructs them to do the opposite of what he has said before. The reason is that the circumstances have changed, thus requiring a change in plans.

Earlier, Jesus had sent out the disciples into the world telling them to carry no purse, no bag, and not even sandals (Luke 10:4)! In that story, Jesus did say he was sending them out like lambs in the midst of wolves. Still, he trusted they would be safe and cared for, needing no extra supplies to drag them down on their mission. But now, only a few chapters later, the plan has drastically changed. Jesus is aware that he now faces the powers of evil at work in the world. He has shared the Last Supper with his beloved disciples and has already predicted that his own best friend, Peter, will betray him three times before morning. Now, he tells the disciples it's time for a new set of rules for a new situation.

At this time, Jesus knows he is being considered among the lawless, and as a result, his followers will be in serious trouble if they don't take extra supplies on their mission. So, this time (Luke 22:35–38), he tells them they'll be needing the purse, the bag, the sandals, and even a sword! He says, "'When I sent you out without a purse, bag, or sandals, did you lack anything?' They said, 'No, not a thing.'" He said to them, 'But now, the one who has a purse must take it, and likewise a bag. And the one who has no sword must sell his cloak and buy one'" (verses 35–36). Things have changed very quickly following the betrayal by Judas, one of his followers. Now the disciples will have to be able to defend themselves or at least move quickly, as their lives are in danger. Many readers are surprised at Jesus' total reversal in instructions to his disciples. Isn't he called the Prince of Peace? What's he doing recommending the purchase of swords? His concern is for their welfare.

Different tools are needed for different times, different strategies for different situations. Jesus is teaching one of life's most difficult leadership lessons: that we must remain flexible, aware, and ready to do what's needed when change comes. Yes, there are times, most times, when our gentleness, openness, and loving spirits are exactly what are required for the situation. But there are also moments when we're called to action, times we must be prepared to deal with enemy forces (forces of evil). There are situations for which the old rules simply do not apply. His previous instructions to them were for different circumstances and for a different time. It would be irresponsible for him to leave them vulnerable and helpless because they were not willing to change.

The disciples answer Jesus saying, "Lord, Look, here are two swords." Jesus responds to them with the words, "It is enough" (verse 38). The disciples seem at first to have understood Jesus, but of course he wasn't really talking about swords. Against the power of the Roman Empire, a few disciples armed with either one sword or even two would amount to no defense at all. Jesus' call for them to arm most likely means that they are to be armed with the power of righteousness, but they must be ready for the worst.

Real life can bring some serious and difficult situations. If leaders think they can carry on the way things were before the problem occurred, then they're likely mistaken. If we think more firepower, more violence, and more buildup of self-defense mechanisms are going to resolve our problems, we're wrong again. Jesus taught the disciples everything they needed to know. On the brink of Jesus' arrest, it seems they still didn't understand much of it. Yet, when he says, "It is enough," he also seemed to be recognizing that he'd have to trust their courage to carry them through.

Most of us have been equipped to some extent to be brave. But there are many ways to be courageous and not any one way is appropriate for all situations. We must learn what we can do and then trust that we will recognize when a situation is in flux, or when change is needed. Will we be ready? Jesus said what he could to prepare the disciples. Now it was up to them to deal with the changes in their situation and work their way through the time of suffering that was ahead for them.

Good Leaders

- are astute at reading the signs of the times;
- find the courage to make needed changes in a timely manner;
- are willing to give instructions that may seem inconsistent with what they have said previously, if these are necessary;
- know there's more than one way to deal with enemies. Always have a Plan B;
- look out for change as it comes so they can be ready for it;
- Make the changes so, if necessary, they can move into the inevitable troubles, not away from them.

Leaders Deal with Change

WHEN OLD TRADITIONS NEED TO BE CHANGED (MARK 7:1-13): RITUAL HANDWASHING

In most organizations, it doesn't take long before traditions arise, and these traditions are nearly always very difficult to break. If they're good traditions, then there's usually no problem. Yet, breaking those traditions is often just what you as a leader may have to do, or at least initiate. Old traditions sometimes hold back progress.

There is a story in chapter 7 of the Gospel of Mark in which Jesus' opponents, the Pharisees, are finding fault with his disciples for not following the tradition of ritual handwashing before eating. In defense of the disciples' behavior in breaking Torah ordinances, Jesus takes the opportunity to teach a life lesson that is especially good for leaders, past and present. The religious leaders in the story want the disciples to wash their hands, their food, and their pots and dishes according to their shared religious tradition. The leaders' intention in this case was to criticize and to monitor everyone's behavior and see to it that other people followed the rules to the letter of the law.

Every leader knows that rules have their place in keeping order. When, as a leader, you try to make changes related to existing rules or traditions, the common response is that people want to keep things exactly as they were in the past (this is compounded when we do the same things the same way year after year). Jesus is by no means against following good traditions or rules. But he is implying that following old rules just for the sake of doing so is a misuse of tradition. We must be aware of the reasons why we engage in our traditional activities. If we've only been doing these things for the sake of tradition and nothing else, then what we're doing may very well have become meaningless. If that is the case, it's very likely time for a change.

Good Leaders

- are open to new ideas and willing to put away old traditions when necessary;
- focus their energies on worthwhile purposes;
- know that rules have their place but only when the reasons are good;
- know we need to understand why we are following traditions and doing things;
- care for the nourishment of spirits as well as of bodies.

Chapter IV

Leaders Deal with the Negative

It's an unfortunate fact that things don't always go well. It's not the negative things themselves but the way we handle them as leaders that make the difference. The negative, at best, can be turned around full circle into something positive. But this is not always possible. More often, the best we can do is to handle the negative with grace. In this section, we will consider a variety of situations in which Jesus had to deal with negative forces.

MAKE REPRIMANDS SHORT AND HONEST (MARK 4:35–41): CALM THE SEA

Reprimanding a person is never a pleasant task, but at times, it is a necessary one. The best way to deal with reprimanding, as it is with praising, is to make your words short and honest. The person needs to face what he or she has done wrong, but this does not require a lengthy dissertation. The act of criticism is often embarrassing for both parties, so the quick and clear method works best. Jesus was not one to criticize individuals although there were times when he had plenty to say about "this generation" or about certain religious groups who opposed him. Still, there is one example of a short and honest reprimand on his part in the well-known story of the calming of the sea in the Gospel of Mark. The evening had come, after a busy day. Jesus wants to go over to the other side of the lake, so he and the disciples get into a boat. A strong windstorm kicks up, as is common on small lakes, and things are looking dangerous. Jesus, like Jonah in the book of that title, is asleep on a cushion at the stern of the boat, not seeming to be concerned at all for their welfare. They wake him, sounding a bit rude but probably just nervous and scared, saying, "Teacher, do you not care that we are perishing?" (verse 38). Jesus gets up calmly, quiets the storm, and then offers them a short honest reprimand, saying, "Why are you so afraid? Have you still no faith?" (verse 40). Notice that he doesn't say, "How dare you talk to me like that?" That would be getting personal. He is simply taking note that all that he has done and said in their presence up to this point appears to have been in vain. They don't get it! Do you see how powerful and constructive a short honest reprimand can be?

Notice also that Jesus does not call the disciples bad names or suggest in any way that they are bad people. He hits instead on the two issues that are the most important of what he has been trying to teach them and has been continually demonstrating to them: they should not be afraid, and they should have faith. It's that simple. They would not have been offended by his reprimand because they trusted him and understood that he had their best interests in mind. After all, before he even began to go after them, he had already calmed the storm on their behalf and, thereby, had made sure they were safe. They must have known they were in good hands.

Good Leaders

- recognize the need for and the importance of reprimands to keep things on course;
- make reprimands short and honest;
- criticize the behavior or the action, but never the person.

KNOW TO SAY NO (LUKE 8:26-39): THE MAN MADE SANE

Today, it's extremely popular to tell people to never say no. Those who lead are often advised to first say yes to everything and, later, decide whether to do it. It's true that most people don't like to hear the word "no." For many years, we've been taught that good negotiating techniques are those that get all parties to "yes." Books and counseling methods remind us that we're all OK. And more and more games are being created in which there is less real competition so that, as the old carnival barkers used to put it, "everybody plays; everybody wins." These methods have surely built self-esteem across the board and, in general, have improved life for many. Still, we can learn a powerful lesson from a story in which Jesus seems perfectly comfortable in saying no.

The narrative about the so-called demoniac in the Gospel of Luke is graphic. Jesus arrives in a cemetery-type area where he comes upon a man described as demon possessed. The Gospel writer recounts the seeming hopelessness of the man's situation. When we first encounter this man, he is said to be flailing about among the tombs, cutting and hurting his body, and clearly being a danger to himself and others. He is not in his right mind. Jesus confronts this man's so-called demons directly. Recognizing Jesus' true identity, the demons flee from the man, leaving him in his right mind. So far what we have here is a dynamic and dramatic healing story that tells about Jesus' power over the forces of evil, the main message of the story. But if we're looking for leadership lessons, we can see them here as well, in what follows.

Sometime later, this same man is found "sitting at the feet of Jesus, clothed, and in his right mind" (verse 35), quite the opposite picture from what he had been when Jesus first encountered him. Now, apparently totally sane, the man begs Jesus to be allowed to go along with him. It appears the man has decided to become a disciple. He seems almost to assume that he's invited. Jesus, however, has other plans for the man and proceeds to redirect him. Jesus simply says no; the man cannot go with him. He is to return instead to his own people and tell them what God has done for him. The man does what he's told.

There is a leadership lesson in Jesus' decision here. The man has asked to go with Jesus, and Jesus has clearly turned him down. Why? In other cases, Jesus seems quick to say, "Follow me." We can't know the motives behind this choice, but I offer some possibilities. First, it might be that Jesus has discerned this man can be most useful back home with his own people. We all work best in an environment we're accustomed to and with the people we know well and who know us. When change happens for the better in our lives, when we improve or change in some good way, who is likely to recognize and appreciate the change in us better than those who knew us before? The people who have known us for so long, admittedly, are not always quick to accept our positive change. Still, our improvements cannot really go unnoticed over time if we return to our people and stay with them! The best place for us to be is in a setting where we can continue to grow and participate in making things better for others. On our own turf we can best demonstrate the very good news that change for the better really can happen. Back with our own people is not always the place we think we want to be. And, of course, back home is not the place to which all of us are sent. But Jesus as a good leader knew best where this particular man ought to be planted. The once demon possessed man proves he is truly cured and in his right mind when he obeys Jesus' instructions and is willing to go back to his own people. Eventually, they would rejoice when they understood how he had changed. They would realize then that they, too, could change and that real healing could happen at many levels. For all this to take place for everyone's good, Jesus had first to say no!

Another strong leadership lesson here may seem tough. It is possible that the man was ready to go home but that he still may not have been ready to go with Jesus—that is, to move in a completely new direction. People may be cured of their demons, but that doesn't mean their transformation is instantaneous, or even complete. In most cases we and those we lead are in process; none of us are finished yet. Further growth is required. When Jesus is ready to move on, he takes with him his chosen disciples, not everyone. He does not take this man who had so recently been completely out of his mind. That does not make the man less valued than others in the larger scheme of things, but Jesus may have decided the man was not yet ready for an altogether new experience. And the choice to go with Jesus is not the man's choice. It's the leader who gets to choose who goes. Whenever possible, leaders should have the choice of who will follow them. Moving forward when we're not ready is seldom a good idea. Others are often in a better position to make those kinds of decisions. Maybe this man was perfectly healed. On the other hand, maybe his real healing had only begun. Healing is a process, and it often takes time before healing turns to wholeness.

Sometimes we can do a lot better for ourselves or others by staying back. Why did Jesus not say, "Come follow me" to this now properly clothed, respectable looking, and well-behaved person? Instead, he turns this man away to do other work on his behalf. It's more important that the man tell his own people about what happened to him than to go off and try to explain his healing to strangers who didn't know him before and would be unlikely to understand. Jesus has loosed him from his bonds so he can go and tell his own people! Like the story of the shepherds in the Gospel of Luke who were the first to receive the good news about the birth of Jesus (Luke 2:16–18), this man has been called not to strangers but to declare good news to his own people.

As a leader, it is seldom easy to say no. Still, there are times you will have to do it. It may or may not be a good idea to explain that your reasons are for the greater good. If your negative response to people is for their growth, it's best if you can tell them. Your saying no may even open other doors to them, doors that would otherwise be closed. Still, don't use their growth as an excuse for your saying no, unless that is the legitimate reason for your decision.

Even as a leader, you will also find people who choose to say no to you. When you're not chosen for a promotion, for example, or if the company or group you lead is not picked for a particular project, this doesn't mean others are better than you. It only means you or your project were not needed. In fact, not being chosen should not reflect negatively on you at all.

There are also times when people who work for you, or who follow your leadership, may find it necessary to say no to you. Listen carefully to their reasons. They are likely to be good ones, and it is very possible that you can learn from them.

Good Leaders

- sometimes need to just say no, and it is entirely appropriate;
- know that they (and others) can't always go where they want to go;
- understand that just because they've experienced growth or healing that doesn't mean the growing or healing is complete. It is nearly always a process;
- don't always have to go to an unknown place to fulfill their calling;
- know that when they or their product or service is not chosen it doesn't mean they're not worthy;
- can learn even when their followers say no to them.

DON'T WASTE WORDS (MATT 7:6): PEARLS TO SWINE

It is often a concern of leaders as to how much or how little to speak in a given situation. There's a general impression that great leaders are the ones who say little and always mean what they say. Still, some people just naturally talk more than others, and you have to be yourself. Nevertheless, there are times when there's nothing to be gained by giving yourself away to the wrong people or cause.

It may be waste-of-time talk that Jesus speaks about when, as one item on a list of advice, he says, "Do not give what is holy to dogs and do not throw your pearls before swine, or they will trample them underfoot and turn and maul you" (verse 6). There are times when people will hear what you're saying or recognize the value of what you offer. At other times they will not, no matter how hard you try or how valid your presentation. There are situations in which it's quite simply a waste of time for you to talk, explain, direct, or even present your product. Most of the time, their refusal has nothing to do with you or your motivational gifts. The reason is simply that they are not in the frame of mind to hear you.

Good Leaders

- have a good sense of when their words are likely to be heard and heeded;
- know their audience, and don't waste a lot of time with the wrong audience or the wrong message.

DON'T LET THEM DISTRACT YOU (MATT 16:21-23): NAMING THE DEMON

Have you ever been talked out of doing something that you had planned or that you know is right because there might be danger, uncertainty, trouble, or even inconvenience involved? Sometimes, what may appear on the surface to be the very soul of right or reason is still wrong. At times, the seemingly sensible and logical decisions we make to keep ourselves out of harm's way are the incorrect ones. Even at times when they're not totally wrong, they are still not the best choices.

In Jesus' relationship with his disciples, it is the man Peter (also known as Cephas, Simon, and sometimes Simon Peter) who emerges as the primary of the twelve. Peter is often depicted as sometimes bumbling and confused, but it is his humanness, openness, and ability to bounce back that make readers so fond of him. Leaders, like Peter, often see themselves as far from perfect but are interested and willing to learn from their mistakes. In the sixteenth chapter of Matthew, Jesus has been explaining to Peter that the days ahead are not going to be easy ones, that he (Jesus) is going to be killed and then raised on the third day. His loyal friend Peter seems not to hear the part about Jesus being raised at all. It seems he has stopped listening at the part where Jesus said he'll be in harm's way, and Peter responds strongly. He announces to Jesus that such a thing simply cannot and will not happen! Who would argue with such a demonstration of love and loyalty? One might expect Jesus to respond by saying, "Peter, what a good and trustworthy friend you are showing yourself to be." The reader really expects Jesus to praise Peter. We may even put ourselves in Peter's place, imagining ourselves standing firm and being protective of our precious friend Jesus against all foes! It is for this reason that Jesus' response to Peter hits the reader so hard. It seems to come out of the blue when Jesus replies to him, "Get behind me, Satan! You are a hindrance to me, for you are setting your mind not on divine things but on human things" (verse 23b).

We can assume, of course, that Jesus doesn't mean Peter is the person of Satan. (The term *satan* [in English translations sometimes capitalized and sometimes not] in Hebrew can mean accuser, slanderer, or adversary. The word appears in both Hebrew Scripture [Old Testament] and the New Testament Greek. Satan is mentioned thirty-five times in the New Testament, while the devil [*ho diabolos*] appears thirty-two times. He is also called the enemy, the evil one, and the tempter. In *The Origin of Satan*, Elaine Pagels points out that Satan has power but is not without limitations.[1]) What is Jesus saying, then? He is pointing to the very essence of what and who the Satan really is. Satan or the devil is, at least to some degree at any given time, the one who holds a person back from fulfilling his or her mission and from doing the will of God. The term, *satan*, is being used here as a figure of speech. Jesus is explaining to Peter that when we try to keep others from moving toward good and toward their mission (which, in the case of Jesus

---

1. Pagels, *Origin of Satan*.

here, involves his death and resurrection), then we have fallen into the hands of the evil one, becoming his willing workers.

This is a powerful but difficult life lesson. Yet, if we ask successful leaders who have demonstrated courage in times of danger, trial, or war, they are apt to tell us this message is right on target. Easy and safe roads may keep us protected, but often, they will keep things from changing for the better, and in this manner, they do contribute to sin. In this instance, Jesus was not asking Peter to put himself in jeopardy. He was only asking Peter not to attempt to stop Jesus from fulfilling his own mission and destiny.

Are we as leaders holding others back by keeping them to our own safe standards and our own ideas of how things should happen? As leaders we need to allow, make room for, and encourage good in our midst. We need to stop controlling others, even when it is intended for their protection, and we must make way for their forward movement.

Good Leaders

- can take constructive criticism;
- don't hold others back just to protect them when they need to move forward;
- allow others the space and freedom they need to be creative and courageous and to fulfill their mission.

DON'T LET THEM FOOL YOU (MARK 10:1–9): JESUS RESPONDS TO ADVERSARIES

Most of the time, we can assume that people are being honest with us in our personal lives and in business. Still, it's an unfortunate fact that there are also some out there who are manipulative of others for their own gain. Even good leaders are not always able to discern exactly who these people are, but we must be wise enough to handle situations in a way that we're not tricked by such people.

In the Gospel of Mark, there's a story in which we are told "Some Pharisees came to him, and to test him they asked..." (Mark 10:2 says simply "some," but Matt 19:3 specifies "some Pharisees"). (Because of the way the Gospels were written, it has been a common misconception on the part of Christians that all Pharisees were judgmental, crafty, and arrogant. In fact, the kinds of arguments Pharisees have with Jesus in the Gospels are typical of an acceptable "give and take" that was expected and even enjoyed and celebrated among Jewish religious leaders at the time. The Gospels were written to lift up the name of Jesus. Other characters such as Pharisees and Sadducees who interact with him in the Gospel stories often serve in the narrative as foils to propel the narrative. For this reason, it's important that we look for the point of each text and don't make too many assumptions about the historicity of the story's details, such as the behavior of these groups of leaders.) They asked Jesus a pointed question about whether it was legal for a man to divorce his wife, knowing full well that, according to Scripture, Moses had given permission for a man to write a letter of divorce and then he would be free of her. They must have been assuming they could catch Jesus red-handed. This divorce rule was cruel for women in a time when, without a husband or male relative, a woman whose husband divorced her would be left powerless and poor. What would Jesus say?

Jesus comes up with the perfect answer. He tells them Moses only gave them that rule because the men were so hard-hearted. In fact, he says, God told them differently! Jesus proceeds to quote to them from Gen 1:27b and 2:24 that "male and female he created them. . . . Therefore, a man leaves his father and his mother and clings to his wife, and they become one flesh." Jesus concludes saying, "What God has joined together, let no one separate" (Matt 19:6). Jesus' response is clear, concise, scriptural, and complete.

As leaders we, too, can expect trick questions. We need to practice recognizing them. If those who are asking these questions don't have our best interests in mind, or the interests of the business or group we lead, we must be careful not to fall into their power. We may have a good response like Jesus always did. It is quite acceptable at times for us not to respond at all. We're not required to dance to the tune of others, especially when they are being tricksters.

Good Leaders

- keep alert for trick questions;
- respond without falling into the hands of the tricksters, or choose not to respond.

DEAL WITH FEAR AS A CAUSE OF SIN (REPRISE OF MATT 6:25-34): DO NOT BE AFRAID

There are people who commit what we call sins, people clearly bent on doing wrong because their intentions are evil. They are sick or misled. The best we can do is stay out of their way or try to get them some help. But more often we are dealing with another type who can cause just about as much harm, not because they are evil doers per se but because they operate out of fear. People who are strongly motivated by their own fears are seldom even aware of what harm they might be doing. Yet these people are found everywhere. They wreak havoc, and they can sorely challenge our leadership.

We may think we don't have any fears of our own, but everyone has to some extent. They are those unspoken issues that gnaw away beneath the surface of our lives: that unreasonable fear that we'll be found in some way not to be legitimate; the fear of failure; even (believe it or not) fears that we'll succeed, and our life will change too much. There may be the fear that there won't be enough time to do what we have to do, fear of not being loved, fear that being loved will eventually bring us hurt or sadness, fear that the things we believe in are not so, or that things we don't believe are so. The list of fears goes on. Many people are afraid of death but a lot more fear life! Fear holds us back. It keeps us from embracing the chance to experience the fullness of life. Fear can also cause some people to be actively or passively involved in hurting others.

Jesus repeatedly tells the people not to be afraid. In Matt 6:25–34 he goes into the details of how we worry about clothing and food or about our lives. He admonishes us to realize that we can't change things or make them better by fear or worry. Good leaders understand that fear is often the underlying cause of bad behavior. Most people are proud to some extent, and for this reason do not like to express their fears. There are many ways, as a leader, that you can encourage your people not to be afraid. Like Jesus, you can remind them that there are things they cannot have control over, and they must simply carry on with their lives, seeking what is good and right, and trusting that things will turn out for the best.

Good Leaders

- try to recognize fear in those colleagues, employees, or followers who may be causing trouble, even when those people are hiding it from themselves;
- help people to recognize what they can change and what is out of their hands;
- work to alleviate fears in themselves and others.

WHEN THINGS GET MESSY (MARK 3:31–35): JESUS STAYS WITH THE PROJECT

Most people have good ideas, but when those ideas are questioned or even criticized, many of them will back off, assuming that others know better. Even the best-intentioned friends, relatives, co-workers, and employees may try to get you to change your plans, to get you to do something they think is better, or simply to drop your plan and go home. There are occasions in leadership when you must go ahead with your plan no matter what the responses of others may be. You've made a decision about what needs to be done, and you probably have a good estimate of what the cost will be. Sometimes the price is that others are going to disagree with you, refuse to participate, or even try to thwart your plans.

On one occasion, when Jesus is gathered with his disciples, his mother and brothers come to pick him up and get him out of there. It appears that people have been talking negatively about him, and his mother and family have decided enough is enough. Their intentions to bring Jesus home appear, at first, to be in his best interest. Jesus' response is unexpected. When told his mother and brothers are outside looking for him, he replies by saying, "'Who are my mother and my brothers?' And looking at those who sat around him, he said, 'Here are my mother and my brothers! Whoever does the will of God is my brother and sister and mother'" (verses 33–35). Needless to say, he did not go with them.

The reasons for this story seem to vary in the later Gospel versions, where the writers find more acceptable possibilities than those of Mark. In Mark, it says that the family has come because people are suggesting that Jesus is out of his mind—that is, "For they had said he has an unclean spirit" (verse 30). This could also mean that people thought he was a person of evil intent. The reason for his family's attempting to pick him up would have been to put an end to this kind of rumor, to bring him back home and get him out of the public eye. His immediate family members seem to love him and want what they believe is best for him. They know that, once their Jesus comes home, he will be understood and safe with the people who care about him the most. But he refuses to come with them.

In fact, Jesus uses this potentially embarrassing situation to teach a valuable lesson to those who have chosen to follow him. His words are startling. Jesus lived in a culture very different from our own. Nevertheless, it was much like ours when it came to respect for mothers. (Motherhood still tends to be placed on the proverbial pedestal. Mothers are often viewed as the prototype of worthiness and, in turn, highly honored and respected.) So, we are shocked when Jesus comes up with such a curt response to the announcement that his mother is outside looking for him. We assume that he has broken the cardinal rule of respect for mothers.

For this reason, many cannot hear or understand the meaning of what he says next.

Look at his first statement: "Who is my mother?" Each of us has a birth mother or at least someone who represents a mother figure. We probably love this person with all our hearts. Still, it is also true that all people are what we might call members of one another. Jesus is pointing this out in the strongest way possible, suggesting that all people of goodwill need to care about each other as if they were a family. As mentioned earlier, it is often the case particularly in times of trouble that we tend to grab tight to our own family and all too quickly close ranks. Jesus is pointing out that a better world can never come to fruition under these selfish circumstances. We cannot know for sure, but we might assume he knew his own mother well enough to be sure she'd be the first person to understand what he meant. (According to the Gospel of Luke, Mary, upon finding out she would give birth to the Messiah, utters these words: "Let it be with me according to your word" [Luke 1:38]. Mary appears to have been chosen for this very reason; she, like Jesus, is a prototype of one totally obedient to the will of God.) Too often people choose immediate family at the expense of all others who then get left behind. Jesus courageously teaches, in this instance, that we are all mothers, brothers, and sisters of each other.

Another strong message is also inherent in these words of Jesus. As a courageous leader, he is not afraid of being thought about negatively, as long as his work and goals are honorable. Whatever kind of leadership you are called to do, there will always be naysayers. It seems there are nearly always going to be some who will misunderstand or distrust your motives. This may hurt and annoy you. But good leaders never let this send them home. They say what they need to say, and they remain in the action.

Good Leaders

- stay in the action and don't lose sight of the goals;
- do not let naysayers distract or stop them;

- do not think in terms of "us" and "them," sticking only with their own. They see the larger community as part of the project;
- know that the ideal community is not "top-down."

Chapter V

Leaders Deal with Enemies

Wouldn't it be great if everybody liked us and agreed with our leadership all the time? Leaders know that when we are engaged in our very best work is often the time that the enemies appear and even seem to become more powerful! It may, on their part, simply be jealousy of our success that causes them to be against us. Or there may be fear of competition or just lack of understanding of what we're trying to do. Dealing with adversaries can be a time-consuming business, but deal with them we must. The best thing is to turn them into friends, but that is not always possible. There are times as leaders when we indeed do have to be "wise as serpents and innocent as doves" (Matt 10:16). The world can be a tough place, and we are not expected to be fools.

"BE WISE AS SERPENTS AND GENTLE AS DOVES" (MATT 10:16): JESUS ADVISES THE DISCIPLES

In the tenth chapter of Matthew, Jesus sends his disciples out into the world, even though, as he says, they will be sheep in the midst of wolves. His practical advice for them is that they are to be "wise as serpents and innocent as doves" (verse 16).

The word *shalom*, one of the most important words in Biblical Hebrew, is often misunderstood as simply meaning "peace." Most people want peace in the world, in their families, and in community life, but what is the cost of that peace? Will peace bring joy if it's paid for by buckling in with those who wield power and authoritarian control? The word *shalom* actually means more like "peace with justice."[1] Only when there is some justice can there be any genuine and enduring peace.

Jesus lived his entire earthly life under the yoke of the powerful and oppressive Roman government. Jews were only tolerated because Rome desired to assimilate all the peoples within their territories. So, they allowed Jews to practice their religion. When the Gospel of Matthew was written (around the year 95 CE or later according to many scholars[2]) this was still the case, but there had been a devastating Jewish war, a failed fight for independence. The Jerusalem temple had been destroyed (in the year 70). In many respects, things were even worse than they had been during Jesus' earthly life. Whether the words "be wise as serpents and innocent as doves" actually came from the mouth of Jesus or from a writer remembering Jesus' advice to the disciples, the words were particularly appropriate for the times they would first have been read and heard. The words also offer superb leadership advice for any generation, including ours.

What does it mean to be as wise as a serpent while also being innocent as a dove? Is it even possible? Too often being innocent is perceived as being weak, overly compliant, or blindly obedient. Yet real innocence is also a great virtue. What Jesus calls for in this story that is so challenging is the combination of wisdom and strength with gentleness and sensitivity. Jesus is not criticizing those who are unable to be strong for whatever reason. He is just making sure that his teachings are not misunderstood as

---

1. Prete, "Shalom."
2. Davies and Allison, *Matthew I–VII*, 138.

advocating intentional weakness. Wisdom is power, especially in circumstances where others are wielding power over us unfairly.

Wise as a serpent? In what ways is a serpent or snake seen to be wise? To begin with, most serpents don't sit out in the open air to be a target to their enemies. Secondly, a serpent, when it does decide to make a move, makes that move with lightning speed. Thirdly, it has venom that can destroy the enemy, but it does not always choose to use that venom. Historically, in literature, including the book of Genesis, serpents are perceived to be cunning. Cunning is a quality that is not very acceptable in our society but is found in several biblical texts. Rebekah and her younger son, Jacob, use cunning to trick his father, Isaac, into giving the blessing to Jacob that was reserved for his elder brother, Esau (Gen 27). In the book of Esther, Esther uses cunning by holding dinner parties for her husband, King Ahasuerus, and her enemy, Haman, for the good purpose of saving her people, the Jews, from total annihilation. In the book of Ruth, Naomi conspires with Ruth to be in the right place at the right time so that she has a chance to become the wife of Boaz and, in the process, lift the family name of the deceased husbands of Naomi and Ruth.

So Jesus says, in addition to being wise as serpents, we are also to be as innocent as doves. In other words, any cunning that is needed does not open the door to cruelty or coldness. Perhaps, as leaders, we have not thought much about the importance of innocent gentleness. Yet, if we are doing our job well, there is no reason not to be such.

Good Leaders

- know that cunning, when combined with wisdom and a desire for greater good, may on occasion be appropriate. Nobody asked us to be fools. Rather than allow something bad to happen to ourselves or others, we are sometimes called to employ this kind of wisdom;

- realize that gentleness or innocence is also required, and it will serve us and others well in life.

FIRST, GET THINGS RIGHT (MATT 5:21-26): THE IMPORTANCE OF EVERY RELATIONSHIP

Good leadership, first and foremost, requires good working relationships, and these must be built over time. Jesus understood the importance of getting and keeping relationships right.

Matthew 5:21–26 is a passage seldom preached. The reason may be that the advice of Jesus here is not particularly useful to advance the gathering of financial gifts and tithes to meet church budgets! He says, "So when you are offering your gift at the altar, if you remember that your brother or sister has something against you, leave your gift there before the altar and go; first be reconciled with your brother or sister, and then come and offer your gift" (verses 23–24). This suggests that we make our relationships right first because it is only then that our gift to God will be acceptable. There's an adage for married couples that we all know. It says, "Never go to bed mad," but Jesus' courageous statement says in effect, "Never go to worship mad." If not this exactly, at least the text suggests that our gifts are of little interest to God, and will have no efficacy on our behalf, if we have not first straightened out our human relationships.

Here's a simple lesson for living and for leadership. Jesus is pointing out that the gift most pleasing to God is right relationships among people. Thus, we are required to take the time and energy needed to recover any relationships that might be in jeopardy, as well as any which already seem lost, and to restore friendships and kinships. Once our interpersonal relationships are reestablished, only then can we get on with the rest. This is also the case in business.

It's difficult to be a leader when we're not on good terms with all the people we lead, as well as with our colleagues and even our competitors. One reason is that, unfortunately, there is no shortage of people who like to take random pot shots at their leaders. This may be out of petty jealousy or due to other issues the person may be dealing with that don't even relate to the leader directly. We can't make everyone happy all the time. Still, it's important to mend fences when we can and to at least know we've done all we can to make things right.

Once that work is completed, we're bound to be better leaders because we will feel good about ourselves. This, as Jesus has pointed out, is really the starting point. It is a fact that you'll make little progress as a leader when you're troubled with too many unresolved disagreements with others. Once these relationships are made right, you will be able to concentrate fully on the tasks at hand and, of course, expect more cooperation from colleagues and followers.

Good Leaders

- are more comfortable when they know they've done their best to make and keep right relationships;
- understand that "sacrifices" mean little if relationships are not in order.

SETTLE OUT OF COURT (LUKE 12:57–59): JESUS ADVISES THE CROWDS

How many leaders have found themselves in the middle of a lengthy and expensive court case and wished with all their heart they'd never let the thing get started in the first place? Even thinking about the possibility of litigation can be very upsetting to most people. The matter of who is guilty and who is innocent is often the least of our problems once we're faced with the possibility of going to court! The fact is that no matter who is to blame officially, both parties nearly always suffer when the courts are called in to resolve differences. No matter who "wins" financially, it is often the case that, both emotionally and spiritually, all parties lose a lot. One of the reasons is that an animosity tends to build up between the two parties which it might often have been possible to minimize or even avoid if dealt with earlier on. Third parties who enter into the matter between those who are trying to resolve the problem cannot ever really know what transpired. No other person, no matter how much information he or she is armed with, can recreate for a judge or jury what the situation was or explain what all the extenuating circumstances might have been.

In Jesus' time, the Roman law courts must have been enough to put fear into the heart of anyone who was attempting to use them. Jesus makes this practical recommendation: "Thus, when you go with your accuser before a magistrate, on the way, make an effort to settle the case" (verse 58).

The truth is that nobody can write your show for you! No doubt lawyers are often brilliant people. But settling any controversy before the problem escalates can be a far better solution than fighting out issues in a law court.

Good Leaders

- try their best to avoid making adversaries in the first place;
- recognize who their enemies might be;
- make serious efforts to turn enemies to friends when it's possible to do so with integrity;
- stay out of litigation whenever possible;
- work toward mediation if it can be done.

KNOW YOUR ENEMIES (MATT 4:1–11): TEMPTED BY THE DEVIL

Most of us act as if we have no enemies, but leaders nearly always have some formidable adversaries. It's not a good idea to simply pretend they don't exist. If you know who they are, it's usually best to move in toward them, instead of backing away, so you can learn more about them. You can't deal with adversaries if you don't understand them.

Matthew's Gospel offers a strange story in which Jesus is said to have had an encounter with the devil himself! It begins when the devil tempts him. We might expect Jesus to have simply said, "Get away from me," and head out in the opposite direction in short order. Instead in this story, surprisingly, Jesus stays with the devil for quite a lengthy time and allows the devil to lead him all over the place. He also listens carefully to what the devil has to say, and only after hearing each one of the devil's suggestions does Jesus make his brilliant responses.

The first lesson we learn for leadership here is about timing. It's after Jesus has just finished fasting for forty days in the wilderness that the devil shows up to tempt him. This suggests that our temptations often come when we've been experiencing exhaustion or some kind of "wilderness" time, either in our personal or our business lives. In tough times we are more likely to be tempted into some kind of wrongdoing.

The temptations of Jesus by the devil are threefold and connect directly with classic temptations we encounter as leaders.

The first is the temptation to turn stones to bread. That would be taking the easy way out. For Jesus that would have been showing his gifts openly, doing magic instead of teaching.

The second temptation is to throw himself down from the temple, depending on God to protect his Son. The temptation in our case would be to call in special help from those more powerful than we are, instead of working things through humbly and appropriately.

The third temptation of Jesus was to get everything he wanted by succumbing to worship the devil. This, in our time, is the temptation to sell ourselves for whatever gains can be made, without consideration that we would be, in fact, selling out!

In each of the above listed temptations, Jesus responds to the devil by saying no to him, but in each case he also does so by quoting Scripture. I am not suggesting that good leaders quote

Scripture to deal with their enemies! But, in the case of this Bible story, Scripture is presented as the perfect response a child of God makes when facing evil.

Particularly interesting here is something that few Bible readers notice. In the case of the second temptation, the devil has stepped up the dialogue by choosing to quote Scripture himself. Taking Jesus up to the pinnacle of the Jerusalem temple, the devil suggests that Jesus should throw himself down. He says, directly from Ps 91:11–12, "'For he [God] will command his angels concerning you,' and 'On their hands they will bear you up, so that you will not dash your foot against a stone'" (Matt 4:6). What can we make of this, that the devil is now quoting Scripture in his attempt to tempt Jesus? What a powerful leadership and life lesson there is here. When someone who is against us is trying to get us to do something we do not want to do, that person might have more success when they're speaking "our own language." It's harder for us to say no when the person is speaking something we understand but for wrong reasons, or using terminology that brings us into our comfort zone for the wrong reasons. This is also the case with half-truths. People or organizations that want to convince us of something understand they have to speak our kind of language to entice us. Leaders need to be aware of this. Temptation is easy to resist when we sense the enemies are talking in their own style. But, when they move into the guise of what is familiar to us, we need to be especially careful about what we might be agreeing to.

Interestingly, when being tempted in this way, Jesus did not choose to be particularly creative. He stuck to language that he had long known, words of his own Scripture, probably texts that were memorized as a child. Even though he was very likely exhausted, just having emerged from forty days in the wilderness, he knew he would be able to resist temptation if he stuck to what he knew for sure to be true and right. When we, as leaders, are overworked or in a vulnerable state emotionally, financially, or spiritually, this is not a particularly good time to try to be innovative. It is a time, rather, for us to be steady and hold to things that we know and that we have lived with for a long time.

It is interesting to see in the story that, after three unsuccessful attempts to get Jesus to bend to his evil ways, the devil suddenly departs. If you have enemies, they may also leave once they realize you are not going to play their game.

Good Leaders

- recognize when they're being tempted;
- get to know the enemy with whom they will be dealing;
- try to stick to the steady, tried and true, and known course when being tempted or when overly tired;
- do not bully even though they may have the power or temptation to do so.

Chapter VI

Leaders Deal with Assets

EVEN WHEN YOU FIRST start out as a leader, you will have some kind of assets to deal with. To begin, they may only be your talent or your good team of supportive followers, but in time, these assets will grow, possibly even to a substantial amount that will have to be handled with care. The way that you deal with your assets, be they small or large, will affect your work and your success as a leader. Jesus did not go after money, but he has some serious things to say about how we deal with money and our other assets.

WHO MAKES HOW MUCH? (MATT 20:1-16): WORKERS IN THE VINEYARD

Are you one of those leaders who make decisions about other people's salaries? Or maybe you work for someone else. A lot of people must punch a time clock. As either bosses or employees, most of us have an inner time clock, and we often find ourselves fighting daily against time to accomplish all that we think is required of us.

Everyone expects to give or to get a day's pay for a day's work. It's fair. It's the right thing. It's important for the success of the business, for the movement of commerce, and for the progress of society at large. Who would argue with the total logic of a day's pay for a day's work?

It seems, however, this is not exactly the way Jesus saw it. This concept was created by the world and for the world, and this worldly rule was in full swing in Jesus' day as it is today. And the workday then was likely quite a bit longer than ours. Jesus, it seems, was working with a different set of rules in his parable of the workers in the vineyard. Let's take a look.

He tells the story of a landowner who goes out early in the morning to hire laborers for his vineyard. Several people show up, ready to work. The landowner offers them the "usual daily wage" (verse 2), and they labor for the entire day. But others who also want to work have been trickling in at various times throughout the day, including 9 o'clock in the morning, noon, and even as late as 3 o'clock and even 5 o'clock in the afternoon! To the latecomers the landowner has said he would pay "whatever is right" (verse 4). The "early birds" are shocked and annoyed when they discover, at the end of the day, that these latecomers receive the same pay as they do and are even paid first! It isn't fair. The surprising and challenging message of Jesus here is that it doesn't matter. It is the landowner who's handling the pay, and how much he pays is always his option. If this employer chooses to be generous to those who arrived late, then so be it. When those who worked all day grumble and complain, the landowner explains to them, "Did you not agree with me for a denarius?" (verse 13). He continues, "Am I not allowed to do what I choose with what belongs to me?" (verse 15).

"Now this book has gone too far" you might be saying at this point. How can a leader today who is responsible for financial matters take this kind of advice seriously? The point, however, is not that we are being advised to give money for work not done. The point is this. It is the giver who decides if he or she wants to be more generous to others, perhaps to those who need it the most. Yes, in business, it's good to know what the competition is doing. But their success is theirs. Take your energies and use them for your own work and to build your own successes. If other people worked less but had more success than you, that's really not your business at all.

If you're employed by someone, the salary you agreed to at the beginning is sufficient, and whatever amount you agreed to requires that you give your best. You don't change the rules in the middle of the game. It is the prerogative of your employer to raise your salary in midstream but not for you to ask for more until the time is appropriate (yearly or whatever has been agreed upon in advance). How much money others make for the work they do is simply not your business.

If you're the boss, it is perfectly appropriate for you to raise anyone's salary if and when you deem it appropriate. Don't worry about what the others will think. If they are petty and demand that you act according to their version of what's fair, then maybe they're not the best employees for you anyway.

Theologically speaking, the lesson of the workers in the vineyard (Matt 20) is not about wages or about hours worked. Rather, it's about God's incredible willingness to give us what we do not deserve and did not earn. Is this good news? God may not always seem fair by our human perception of fairness. With God, it's never fifty-fifty. We don't get what we paid for or what we earned. We get more because God chooses to be very generous. If God, then, is also generous to others, we are called to rejoice for them but are also called to generosity.

Jesus had the courage in this parable to remind us that God is not adding up points so that the worthiest of us will be invited into God's kingdom. How often we get caught up in trying to be more worthy or more successful than others! Jesus is suggesting that when that kind of principle is in play, there can be no reign of God at work in this world. Also, when we are not willing to share our bounty with others, we're already missing it ourselves.

Good Leaders

- don't waste time comparing others' accomplishments and gains to their own;

- never resent other people's successes;
- seek reward only according to what they've earned. But they're not surprised when they receive much more;
- don't judge how much their boss does for others. It's not their business.

WHAT BELONGS TO WHOM? (LUKE 20:20-26): RENDER UNTO CAESAR

As leaders, there are always powers that need to be dealt with. The government, for example, has its requirements of all of us. Who likes to pay taxes? A ridiculous question. Still, in return for our portion of taxes paid, there are also services rendered. If we realize that the paying of taxes is the sharing of the responsibility toward the society we live in, we can feel better about it. It's not lost money. Rather, it is money spent for services promised and (hopefully) services rendered. So, our responsibility as good leaders is to be sure we pay the correct amount and, of course, that we don't, by mistake, pay too much.

First century Jews, at the time of Jesus, surely enjoyed paying taxes even less than we do. History indicates that they were highly overtaxed and, of course, that they had no voice in the Roman government that ruled them. We can learn a most interesting leadership lesson from Jesus in this regard. Spies were sent to challenge Jesus by asking him whether it is lawful to pay taxes to the emperor or not. It is clearly a trick question. If Jesus were to speak against paying taxes, he could have found himself in serious trouble with the Romans. If he said it was acceptable to pay the taxes, he may have been perceived by his own people, the Jews, as being pro-Rome, and Rome was the enemy. (The most despised people of any nation under occupation are often those who assist the enemy in oppressing their own people.)

Jesus asks the adversaries to show him a coin. He inquires of them as to whose picture is on the coin. The answer of course is that of Caesar. Then he says to them, "Give to Caesar the things that are Caesar's, and to God the things that are God's" (verse 26). What a brilliant show of leadership. Even after being entrapped, Jesus has not only extricated himself but has also taught a practical lesson. It seems there are always going to be taxes, and there are always going to be requirements to be met in order to participate in our society, whatever political systems hold sway. We don't have the option to opt out. We are always part of the big picture in a very real world. We have obligations that are required by society, local, state, and federal governments.

Have you thought about what parts of you may belong, at least partly, to something that is bigger than yourself? What about your time and talents? What about your loyalty and love? We might think at first that Jesus should have told the people not to pay their taxes to Caesar. After all, Caesar was an oppressor and the enemy. There are two reasons why Jesus would not do this. First, he surely knew it was a trick question which, should he have come up with an anti-Caesar answer, would have sent him quickly to jail! Secondly, in his response, he was acknowledging that we must work within the confines of the situation we find ourselves in. This was learned by the people of Israel while they were in Egypt (until the time of their liberation with the exodus) and then again during their exile in Babylon (586–538 BC). There were also many who chose to stay in the diaspora even after liberation was presented to them as an option. Much has been written about how they learned to live and thrive under difficult enemy sovereigns and oppressive governments.

Another example of "rendering unto Caesar" is found in the story of Hagar, in Hebrew Scripture (Old Testament). Sarah gets her husband, Abraham, to send his concubine, Hagar, out into the wilderness with her small child (Gen 16). When the angel of the Lord came to her, the message was not, "I will save you now," but rather, "Return to your mistress and submit to her. . . . I will so greatly multiply your offspring that they cannot be counted" (Gen 16:9b–10). Hagar would have preferred to be free, but she was advised to go back to the home of her oppressors for the sake of the survival of herself and her child. She was promised good things would come to her at a later time. Sometimes we must pay a high price and be patient so that we can simply continue another day.

Our life and our leadership skills now may be far from perfect. Also, there may be any number of reasons why we're not completely free or liberated right now. What we must do is live the best way we know how, never forgetting where our true allegiances lie. Then, rooted in right, we will get through current circumstances until there comes a better opportunity for us.

Good Leaders

- render to those in power what is required, including paying taxes honestly;
- always remember that their first loyalty is to do what is right;
- are willing to wait for what they need, if necessary, until times are better.

DON'T SAVE YOUR LIFE, SPEND IT (LUKE 12:13–21): MR. BIGGER BARNS

Many of us have been raised with the idea that we should gather and hold on to our resources as much as we possibly can. Maybe if we hang on tightly to our goods, our money, and our talents, we will eventually have enough to be what we consider to be wealthy or successful. But it may be that just the opposite is true. Good leaders know they need to take assets and spend them, invest them, or use them for good purposes.

Jesus offers a parable in which a man builds up his own private personal empire, trying to protect himself but not realizing he is about to die. He has put all his treasure in the wrong places. He somehow missed the fact that there were things even more important than his own earthly security. Grabbing and holding on to possessions could never bring him true happiness and, ultimately, could not keep him alive.

We do not choose what moment we're going to die, and no amount of money can change the time or the way we will die, but

Leaders Deal with Assets

we can change the way we choose to live. Mr. Bigger Barns had somehow determined that the accumulation of his wealth was what determined his worth. It's difficult for most of us to think about, but from birth, all of us are already in some state of dying. Today's society has arranged it so that we can avoid thinking about our death for most of our lives. Even when very elderly people die, their families quite often act surprised, sometimes even shocked. Why is everyone so unprepared? Death comes to us all, if not sooner, then later. Mr. Bigger Barns was working under the assumption that the more he owned the safer he would be. This, of course, had never been the case.

Do we miss a major point here? Was this person's life not worth more? Did he squander his life? William Wordsworth, in his poem "The World Is Too Much with Us," says it well: "Getting and spending, we lay waste our powers." Most of us are required or expected to spend a good deal of our lives earning a living. We are expected to be responsible for ourselves and our families. This is a valid enterprise. What Jesus is saying is that there's much more to life than making money and acquiring riches. We are not to be hoarders! Rather, we need to use money responsibly and also to share any bounty that our labor has provided.

How different Mr. Bigger Barns's life would have been if he'd spent at least some portion of his wealth providing and caring for others and giving his time and talents! He would very likely have been a better and a happier person. Perhaps even his eternal life was in jeopardy for not having shared and given more, but the Scripture doesn't say this. It speaks rather of this man's personal loss. His time on earth is gone. His days have been used up in gathering worldly things, and now it's too late to share or enjoy life. He cannot retrieve his life. He also can't say he's lived it as well as he might have. His opportunities are now gone. His time has run out.

In addition, Mr. Bigger Barns might be said to have exhibited a lack of faith, a lack of trust. Why would a person want to store up more resources than what were needed? Jesus teaches in the Lord's Prayer that we're to ask God to "give us today our daily bread" (Matt 6:11). Our needs for the day are sufficient. This is a hard lesson, and it takes great trust on the part of those who would follow Jesus to believe and act in a way that indicates they trust that God will provide for their future.

As leaders, we understand that we must exercise good judgment in how much we keep for ourselves of what we've earned or built up in a business. There needs to be some element of giving and sharing. This is understood now by many of the world's wealthiest people, who are known to apportion percentages of their earnings to any number of worthy causes. Giving away a portion of our bounty is good for business. It also affords the giver a strong sense of participation in society at large, not to mention a good night's sleep!

Good Leaders

- don't hang onto things too tightly;
- allow themselves to grow by giving instead of hoarding;
- believe in others and believe in tomorrow.

BE GRATEFUL TO THE PROVIDER / RESPECTFUL OF THE MESSENGER (MATT 21:33-44): RENTERS IN THE VINEYARD

Even if we are the boss or CEO, there is much that we do not and cannot own. We may even own the building or own the business, but we don't own people. As mentioned earlier, we still have to pay our taxes. In addition, our business depends on many factors, such as good weather for growing crops, trucking companies to deliver our goods, workers' unions that guide our workers, and such. Even if we literally own the place or own the business, most of us can be called "renters" in one or more aspects of our leadership role. To some extent, we are dependent on others.

Jesus tells a story of how badly some renters of a vineyard treated the landlord and his son (Matt 21:33-34). This narrative is a tough one to read. All the landowner is asking for in this story

Leaders Deal with Assets

is the rent that is due to him. Instead of paying, the renters cause mayhem, in the end even killing the landowner's son who has come to collect the rent. Not only misbehavior but violence can come at times from people we are only trying to serve.

Those of us who own something usually take pretty good care of it. Those who are just passing through tend to care for it less. As leaders, we need to show deep respect for any materials, any ideas, and especially any people who are being loaned to us.

For those who work for someone who's been put in charge, there is a tendency on the part of workers, much like the renters in the parable, to spend a good deal of time challenging that person's authority and decisions. Nobody has to accept hierarchical behavior or actions in our free society, but when others have been placed in leadership positions over us, why are we so seldom willing to let them lead?

There is also a problem encountered by the "rent collectors" of this world. Because they represent the owner, the "renters" too often don't allow them to do their job. The old cliché about "killing the messenger" is still true. The messengers need to be allowed to do their work in peace. Too often in business, as in this story, we beat up the messenger.

What we have here is a parable about squandering the gift of life by being petty, selfish, and cruel. It is about profound disrespect for the provider of all that is good.

Good leaders

- know their opportunity to lead is a gift and they don't take it for granted;
- recognize that none of us really "own the place";
- let people do their work;
- don't blame the messenger when the news is what we don't want to hear.

YOUR BEST ASSETS ARE YOUR BEST PEOPLE! (MARK 5:22-24, 35-42; 9:2-8): JESUS CHOOSES THREE

It doesn't take long for those who lead to realize that certain of their followers, their group, or their team have special gifts for the tasks at hand. These people naturally seem to rise above the crowd, probably because they have found their calling, which makes their work seem more like pleasure. If these people are not obvious to you as a leader, it's possible you don't have any such people, or that you have not been looking. Keep your eyes open for the gifted ones. They're not necessarily the ones who've been making special efforts to impress you. They too have their place, but the truly gifted are a different lot. They will do you proud and need to be nurtured.

The Bible offers a really good example of Jesus in this regard. The ninth chapter of Mark tells us that "Jesus took with him Peter and James and John and led them up a high mountain apart, by themselves" (Mark 9:2). This is a strange and mystical story. On the mountain, Jesus is transfigured and seen by the others to be talking with the two greatest biblical characters of the past: both Moses and Elijah!

For such a spectacular event, why didn't Jesus bring along all twelve of his disciples, or, for that matter, the crowds of interested people who were following him? It is very possible that, whatever this mysterious mountain experience might have been, Jesus understood that it was only these three of his hand-chosen followers who would be capable of understanding it. As it turns out, even they appear to have been confused. Peter expressed his desire to build booths to hold onto their three heroes, Jesus, Moses, and Elijah, but realized that was not the appropriate response to what he had experienced. As they came back down the mountain, Jesus did some explaining to the three but also admonished them to tell no one what they had seen until after his resurrection. Whatever it was that happened to them up there on the high plain, it is clear that not everyone would be able to handle or interpret what they had experienced.

There is yet another excellent example of Jesus choosing only a small group. In the fifth chapter of Mark, a little girl is said to have already died. Her father, Jairus, a synagogue leader, calls Jesus in to revive and heal the child. Again, as in the story of the transfiguration, Jesus chooses these same three disciples, Peter, James, and John (Mark 5:37), along with the parents, and no one else, to go in to the child's bedside. There, he revives her and, as in the story of the transfiguration, admonishes those who were present to tell no one. This healing is apparently something he feels that they, but not others, are going to understand.

As leaders, we hold a lot of information. We also engage in a good deal of dreaming and planning for the future that we may choose to keep to ourselves. It's good if we can share some of the responsibility. We can't hold it all inside, and we also can't tell everything to everybody. We may want to choose a small number of our most talented people and give them the honor of carrying with us some of the responsibility of knowing the big picture, along with the plans and the dreams for the future.

Good Leaders

- carefully choose those with whom they will share the most important information;
- decide what of their own hopes, dreams, and plans they want to tell these people.

USE WHAT YOU'VE GOT (MATT 25:14–30): DON'T BURY THE MONEY

It is a fact that money is for spending! So are talents. When these are hidden under a barrel, so to speak, they do no good for anyone. It is the work of good leaders to wisely invest both. If you are no financial wizard, then as a leader you'll have to learn as much as you can about how money works. It is our responsibility to do what's best with all our assets. In addition, what special gifts have you and those you lead been given? Are you using them fully? Better yet, are you using them for good?

Jesus tells a story about how a certain amount of money is dispersed among three servants while the landowner goes away. Those who choose to invest and use the money manage to do quite well. When the owner returns, he finds that one servant has chosen to bury money that was placed in his care. That person is seriously reprimanded by the owner for not having brought the money forward and invested it. At first, it doesn't seem fair. What's wrong with his having protected what belongs to the owner? He didn't gamble away the cash and he didn't lose it. He only tucked it away safely so that it would be there for sure, to be given back intact when the owner returned. The problem was that he played it safe at the owner's expense. And he didn't use what was given to him to make something better.

When we are entrusted with personal talents, they too are meant for using, not for holding back. There is another Bible story, this one in the book of Revelation. It is written as a letter to the church of Laodicea from an angel. The letter says, "So, because you are lukewarm and neither cold nor hot, I am about to spit you out of my mouth. For you say, 'I am rich, I have prospered, and I need nothing.' You do not realize that you are wretched, pitiable, poor, blind, and naked" (Rev 3:16–17). These are strong words about the mistake of playing it safe, of being unwilling to commit, metaphorically being neither too hot nor too cold. Most of us have plenty of assets and talents. Our provider, God, has been generous with us. Now we, as leaders, should not waste, hide, or misuse the gifts that have been so freely bestowed on us. If you think you may not know what all your talents are, it's probably time to find out by trying things. If you know what your assets and gifts are, and you've been hiding them away, it's time to bring them out and use them to be a better leader who works for a better world.

Good Leaders

- understand that money, as well as assets of all kinds, are to be used;
- are not stingy;
- use money and talents wisely, to the best of their abilities;
- are courageous and generous in their dealings;
- don't always play it safe;
- encourage others to use their talents and assets.

Chapter VII

Leaders Encourage Others

We all know we should be encouraging of others, but what are the best ways to do this? Jesus was a great role model, so let's look at some of his ways of being an encouraging leader. Some of them may surprise us.

WHAT'S GOOD FOR ONE MAY NOT BE GOOD FOR THE OTHER (LUKE 10:38–42): MARY AND MARTHA

Hard work is honorable and praiseworthy, but it takes special courage to stop along the way to listen, learn, and grow. Leaders should be sure to include not only the practical, but also beauty and culture in their lives. And, for busy leaders, continuing study has to happen as well. All these must take place and not be passed up when the opportunities present themselves even if there never seems to be time for them.

Jesus visits two sisters, Mary and Martha. Early in the visit, Martha reprimands Mary, who has chosen to sit and listen and learn from Jesus while Martha busies herself making things ready in the kitchen. Countless Christian women today say they see themselves as the Marthas of this world, the workers. They are not sure what to make of it that Jesus seems to defer to Mary and her choice to sit at his feet while Martha works so hard at taking care of the needed basic hospitality.

A few words on good Martha's behalf! Surely, both Jesus and Mary were aware that, in principle, Martha was right. Mary should properly be in the kitchen or wherever it is that she can work with Martha and do her share of the labor. The world has a lot of rules, written and unwritten, about such behavior! Courteous people are expected to work together so that no one person has to carry the burden. It's not long before the Marthas of this world become very annoyed with those Marys who do not participate fully in sharing the work. Mary would soon be in danger of a problem in her relationship with her sister if that day's behavior was to go on for very long! Societies somehow silently dictate these things. It must be remembered, however, that long-suffering Martha is not a total loser in the situation. There is something known as secondary gain, and in being the "nose to the grindstone" hardworking one, the Martha person in every such situation has the satisfaction of being right and usually receives accolades as the one who has proved to be sensible, practical, and a good provider of what is needed in the way of comfort, food, and such.

Mary, on the other hand, has done something vitally important. She has proved to be a risk taker. Knowing full well what her general duties are, she is wise to see that this situation is not usual. Jesus is here *now*. He won't always be here. This is her opportunity to learn from him, to participate, to better herself, or even help make a better world. (To sit at a person's feet was the sign in ancient Judaism of being that person's student.[1])

We can't know what Mary intended (or what the Gospel author intended). But Jesus' response is strong when he says, "Martha, Martha, you are worried and distracted by many things, but few things are needed—indeed only one. Mary has chosen the better part, which will not be taken away from her" (verses 41–42).

---

1. At Acts 22:3, Paul says, "I am a Jew . . . brought up in this city at the feet of Gamaliel, educated strictly according to our ancestral law."

The better part may very well be to sit as a listener and learner instead of always being too busy working. There are, after all, many kinds of work. These sorts of decisions are made every time a person chooses to take the time out for further education, for art, or for culture. When young people are sent off to college, everyone expects them to suddenly get into that "teachable" state, but they're not always in that frame of mind at the time their parents have chosen. Some people decide later in their lives to return to school. When we open ourselves to learning, we enter a state that holds within it the possibility of moving us toward a better understanding and a better life for ourselves and others. In this case, Mary, indeed, chose the better part.

This story about Mary and Martha carries within it an even more important lesson about leadership. Some people have artistic gifts. These people are as capable as anyone of accomplishing the regular daily tasks, the labors of life. But it's not always appropriate that their energies should be depleted doing things that someone else can do just as well. There are times when it is entirely appropriate for the Marthas to defer to the Marys. The Marys, when the time is right and when they're ready, will surely give back to the Marthas and to everyone else a thousandfold. Such a concept is seldom spoken of or written about. It is controversial. It seems to imply that the Marys get privilege for their talent or that the Marthas are being discriminated against. The rule is, of course, that everyone should be treated equally. Maybe so, but without allowing for the special gifts and talents that the Marys in our lives have to share, the world lacks flavor. Jesus showed great leadership when he had the courage to say so.

Good leaders

- know that continuing study, and taking time for culture and art, are important;
- choose a life that includes continuing learning and opportunities for creativity;

- use their talents, not just their elbow grease;
- know it's who they are that counts, not just what they do;
- understand the importance of truly listening to a person;
- know that even when they're right for sure, in some way they may also be wrong;
- encourage others with talent.

DEALING WITH OTHERS' TALENT (JOHN 1:43–53): JESUS AND NATHANAEL

One vital aspect of good leadership is the ability to recognize talent in others. As a leader, it's your business to always be looking for the talents of those who follow you and noting what they do best. They themselves may not even be aware of their best talents.

Jesus' initial encounter with Nathanael is a good example of this kind of leadership work. Their meeting, it appears, is filled with innuendo. One can read this passage aloud in one way and then read it again with a different inflection and come up with an almost opposite interpretation.

First, let us see what's revealed here about Nathanael, his experiences and personality. We see immediately that he is quick-witted and a good speaker. There is one strong hint that he may be an intellectual. Jesus tells Nathanael that he has first seen him under a fig tree. To most modern Christian readers, this indicates nothing more than a location. But to ancient hearers, there would very possibly have been an understanding that Nathanael was an avid student of Scripture. Ancient rabbinic writings indicate that "under the fig tree" is the place where teaching and learning of the Torah was expected to take place.[2] (The word *torah* can mean law, God's divine instruction, the first five books of the Hebrew Scripture and, sometimes, even connotes a large body of interpretation of the traditions related to the laws; known as the Oral Torah.)

---

2. See Prov 27:18, which hints at this when it says, "Anyone who tends a fig tree will eat its fruit, and anyone who takes care of a master will be honored."

We can't tell from the words of the text whether Jesus meant that he literally "saw" Nathanael under the tree or whether he "envisioned" him in his mind's eye in that place. It may be that the writer is suggesting Jesus could discern simply by being present with Nathanael that he studies the holy law and, therefore, that he would be interested in following Jesus and coming to know God better. (In Biblical Hebrew there are separate words for seeing and envisioning, but in Greek the same one is used.) Jesus goes on to tell him, "You will see greater things than these" (verse 50), suggesting that he's pleased with Nathanael. He is pointing out that people who are open to really engage with Scripture and with him in this way are sure to find what they're looking for, and plenty more!

Good Leaders

- recognize and encourage talent in others;
- know the reason for an action may be just as important as the action;
- sense that people understand there's nothing better than feeling understood;
- know that when they're in the right frame of mind, they are open to seeing things they might otherwise not notice.

CHALLENGING OTHERS TO EXCELLENCE (MATT 19:16-26): THE RICH YOUNG MAN

Good leaders can take people further than they thought they could go. But they do not force people to go beyond their strengths.

A rich young man comes to Jesus saying that he wants to know what he must do to obtain the kingdom. When Jesus quotes Scripture, telling him that he need only love God and his neighbor, the man announces that he's already doing all this and has always done so. It's at this point that we begin to suspect the young man has not come for the reason he says. Could it be that he really wanted not to ask Jesus for advice but to show Jesus what a good and religious person he already was? We really don't know. Jesus' answer to him is very likely not what the young man expects. Instead of saying, "Well, you're in, my friend. You've done it all perfectly," Jesus responds to him by telling him how he can go further. He should simply give away all he has and follow Jesus. Now the young man has been pushed beyond what he's willing or possibly able to do. He turns sorrowfully and walks away!

Does Jesus really require that we give away everything we have? Maybe, but it could also be that his intent here was simply to challenge this young person to take the next step in his own growth in faith and in trusting God. In the version of this same story from the Gospel of Mark (Mark 10:17–22) it is added that Jesus "looking at him, loved him" (verse 21). This suggests that Jesus is not displeased with the man, so his teaching is not intended in any way to hurt him but to help. The man appears to have learned that no matter how obedient he may think he is at any given time, he still falls short of what he could be doing. Until he has given up everything, he still has plenty to learn. Until he has recognized and chosen to trust, he has not completely fulfilled God's requirements. It is said that he goes away "grieving" (verse 22). It appears that, indeed, he does understand the lesson, but that he's yet unwilling or unready to make a full commitment.

As long as the commitments we or our followers make are on our own terms, we've very likely not gone the full distance. It is often true that when we think we've done everything we can, we have hardly begun.

Good Leaders

- sometimes may have to work to improve their value system;
- may be surprised how much they're called to do and give;
- value their relationships much more than their belongings.

KEEPING THE PARTY GOING (JOHN 2:1–11): JESUS AT THE WEDDING

As leaders we need to know that enough is not always enough. If we are going to be generous, it ought to be with an overflowing generosity rather than with a careful or calculated one.

The story of the wedding Jesus attends at Cana offers one more dinner party story. Here, Jesus performs his first miracle, not a lifesaving act of healing as one might expect but instead what we might call a "party saving act": providing wine to keep a happy wedding banquet going! Many have suggested over the years that a courteous group of wedding guests simply accepted water as wine to keep their host from being embarrassed. If that were the case, however, that would negate the purpose of this great Jesus narrative.

One point in this story is that our needs are provided for by Jesus, and in abundance. At this wedding, Jesus does not just give a needed or even appropriate amount of wine. No! He comes up with what amounts to approximately one hundred and eighty gallons of the best wine! Point: God is generous! God celebrates with us.

Also, we see that Jesus found a wedding party to be a valid occasion for a miracle, his first miracle. He understood that people need to be more than just OK. They need to be happy.

A second issue is that of timing. Jesus had already told his mother, who was present with him on this occasion, that his time had not yet come. Why then would he go ahead with the miracle of providing the wine right then? The answer may simply be that it was needed. The message for us here comes from his actions rather than his words. He is willing to provide for the need in spite of his own agenda or his own planned timeline. How often do we choose our own schedule for our generosity toward others and find ourselves unable or unwilling to be flexible when people need us the most? Jesus teaches by example that even the most important agenda (what could be more important than his own agenda?) or the best laid plans may have to be changed to nourish those who thirst! The result of this particular story was a magnificent party, a joyful banquet that did not have to end too soon!

Good Leaders

- remember that it is good to be generous;
- don't think too small;
- stay flexible and remember that plans can change. They may have to be generous at a time they did not plan.

ALLOWING FOR THE SUCCESS OF OTHERS (LUKE 9:49–50): ANOTHER HEALS IN JESUS' NAME

It seems that, at least in the business world, competition prevails. When the winner is not you, you will be disappointed. You may also harbor some negative feelings toward those who win. It may not be easy to change your feelings, considering there has been some aspect of defeat on your part. Yet, a sincerely positive attitude toward the success of others is a real asset for good leaders.

Jesus' disciple John says to him, "'Master, we saw someone casting out demons in your name, and we tried to stop him because he does not follow with us.' But Jesus said to him, 'Do not stop him, for whoever is not against you is for you'" (verses 49–50). Think of the number of answers Jesus might have chosen to give. He could have said, "You should have reprimanded the man if he's not doing things the way I teach!" Or he might have said, "Go back and tell that man to stop immediately." Instead, Jesus graciously lets it go, explaining that the man is doing them no harm and, at least to some degree and in his own way, is following them.

Pettiness is, at the least, unattractive and, at worst, destructive. Leaders need to guard against exhibiting any signs of jealousy. Other people in similar businesses or groups to our own are not our enemies. It is often the case that we have in common with them the work or the project that we care about the most. So, in some sense, we're colleagues with them, even if the other parties may not feel that way. When competitors perceive each other as enemies, everybody loses. It's likely that we'll win some and lose some. When others succeed, we can afford to celebrate for them and maybe even with them. Who knows? We may need each other someday.

Good Leaders

- rejoice with others who do well and who accomplish good things;
- concentrate efforts and energies on their own work and on doing their best, without jealousy.

KEEP COMMUNICATIONS OPEN (JOHN 20:19-29): THOMAS SEES JESUS' WOUNDS

Keeping communications open is a vital component of successful leadership. It's so easy to assume that we must decide what our people should and should not hear and know about, thinking we know best. And, too often, we are surprised when we find that people are hurt or confused because they have not been "in the loop."

There's a beautiful story in the Gospel of John that tells how Jesus, after his death, returned to a gathering of the frightened disciples to calm their fears. One disciple, Thomas, was not present when Jesus appeared. We know this man as "doubting Thomas" because he tells his friends he refuses to believe that Jesus who died is now alive again. He says, "Unless I see the mark of the nails in his hands and put my finger in the mark of the nails and my hand in his side, I will not believe" (John 20:25). Our immediate reaction is that Thomas is asking for too much. He should not have made this demand. His friends had seen the proof, and this should have been enough for him. So, we are surprised when, on the occasion of Jesus' next visit, he gives Thomas exactly what he wants. He says to Thomas, "Put your finger here and see my hands. Reach out your hand and put it in my side. Do not doubt but believe" (verse 27). Certainly, Jesus didn't have to do this, but the story tells us that he chose to! Why? We can guess that Thomas may have decided eventually that he'd believe anyway. But Jesus wanted to be sure Thomas got what he needed and knew everything he needed to know. Jesus then reminded all of them that there would be many people in the future who would never be able to see any such proof about his resurrection but would decide to believe anyway.

Jesus chose to keep the communication with Thomas wide open. As leaders we must remember that misunderstandings can cause an incredible amount of harm. Open communication has become a hallmark of great leadership. It costs nothing and its value cannot be counted.

Good Leaders

- don't hide the really important information;
- try to keep all communications open whenever possible;
- at times, have to go out of their way to be sure people are informed.

KEEP ON TRYING (LUKE 5:1–11): GOING FISHING AGAIN

Most people who have been successful have learned that they should not give up too soon. Thomas Alva Edison is said to have made thousands of failed attempts before he created the first successful light bulb. Now, we can't imagine life without electric lights. There are so many times that we stop just short of accomplishing our goals or our mission and never even realize it.

Jesus was standing by the water. The fishermen were washing their nets after a failed day of fishing. Jesus has taken one of the boats for a while to use as a kind of speaking platform where he could talk from just a short distance offshore to the crowds who gathered to hear him. Now he tells the fishermen, to their surprise, to put out again to deeper water and make another attempt to catch some fish. They reluctantly agree. This time, to their great surprise, there is a huge catch. It turns out it was not too late after all, as they had thought. Jesus takes this opportunity to tell them they soon will be fishers for people!

Leaders and their people work hard and often get very tired after a long day's work. There are times they're quite sure they've done everything they can. But most of us are much stronger than we think and often have more energy than we ever dreamed we had. There are times when it can be a very good idea to get back into the boat and have another try!

Good Leaders

- have or acquire a good sense about how much they and their people can do—and it's sometimes much more than they had anticipated;
- don't give up too soon;
- keep on believing that things will work out for the best.

BUILD ON THE STRENGTHS (LUKE 19:1–10): JESUS DINES WITH ZACCHAEUS

In business and in life, it's often far too easy to find fault in others (and in ourselves) and dwell on the problems and not the possible solutions. Leaders can make real progress when they're willing to put away the negative so they can take the time to build up the strengths of themselves and those who follow them.

There is one good story about building on strengths that's found only in the Gospel of Luke. Jesus enters a town called Jericho. In that place there is one man who is determined to get a look at him. Zacchaeus is a little guy—that is, short in stature! He is despised by everyone because he has an important but highly unpopular job; he's a tax collector. Tax collectors in Jesus' time were notorious for graft, not to mention the fact that they worked for the Romans, who were already taking more in taxes than the Jewish people could bear. Still, Zacchaeus did have some attributes. We can tell from the wording of the story that he had a lot of energy, so much so that it is said he "ran ahead and climbed a sycamore tree to see him [Jesus]" (verse 4). As Jesus is coming by, he spies him up there. Jesus promptly invites himself to dinner at the man's home. It isn't long before Zacchaeus has already announced to Jesus that he's going to give half his possessions to the poor. In addition, if anyone has been defrauded by him in the past (and we can guess they have), he promises to pay back four times what is owed.

How could Jesus have guessed that little man would do such a thing? He saw something special in this man Zacchaeus because he chose to pull him out of the crowd. Here, he could see, was a person who would run and climb a tree just to get a peek at him. When Jesus got to his house, he had every chance to reprimand him for what were surely his many faults. Zacchaeus, after all, had been working for the enemy and taking advantage of his own people! Instead, Jesus had picked him out of all the others who were on the street that day, to share a meal with him. Jesus, by the mere fact of having invited himself to dinner, has shown the little man that he cares about him and that God cares as well. In return, Zacchaeus has chosen to take the high road and tell Jesus he is going to make things right in his life. Having seen Zacchaeus's burst of energy and strong desire to simply get a look at him, Jesus has built on the man's initial desire to see him. He has made it possible for Zacchaeus to make these huge life-changing decisions. These will not only change Zacchaeus but also will work to the advantage of the poor and any others he may have cheated or treated wrongly in the past. Jesus has built on the man's strengths instead of dwelling on his failures in the past.

Good Leaders

- don't waste time dwelling on the negative;
- keep an eye open for those who are ready to change for the better;
- build on the strengths of others as well as on their own strengths.

Chapter VIII

Leaders Move Forward

ONCE YOU'VE BECOME A good and successful leader, you realize you can't remain static, doing the same things in the same way. You need to keep on growing, and this means to be continually moving toward new horizons. The world is ever changing, as discussed earlier, and we must be changing with it. Jesus was always heading in a direction. Let's look at some examples that can be useful to our leadership.

WHEN TO BREAK THE RULES (MARK 2:23-28): JESUS HEALS ON THE SABBATH

The world and the workplace seem to be populated with two distinct types of people. Let's call them, for the sake of this discussion, the *process* people and the *order* people. Both types are vital to any workplace, but they rarely understand each other. The *order* people are sometimes, in jest, named the *bean counters*, but we need *bean counters*. These are those good people who make sure everything is in its place and that things are going according to the budget, the plan, the schedule, and always accomplished in the proper order.

In the meantime, the other group (the *process* people) is the one always looking to the future, adjusting to new realities in the present and, in the process, often unknowingly causing a good deal of disruption to those *order* folks!

The old adage "Rules were made to be broken" doesn't really explain or resolve the problem of what to do about those rules. If they are made to be broken, then what good are they? If they can never be broken, rules can be dangerous. How do you function as a leader when rules you may yourself have created are being broken? And what do you do when it must be you who needs to break those same rules that you or others have created to make things work better? When Jesus' disciples break the religious rules of their time by eating grain on the Sabbath, they do it because they're hungry. Jesus, a *process* person, is immediately accosted by the *order* people, who promptly remind him that there are rules! In response, Jesus argues that according to Scripture, even David and his men had eaten holy bread from the temple because they were hungry. There's a practical lesson here. Rules are important and they have their place, but sometimes other matters take precedence.

We can almost hear the naysayers wondering what would happen if everybody decided to break the rules. They would assume the result would be chaos. Jesus understood, however, that there are times for "field expediency," and this was one of those times.

On another occasion, Jesus was even criticized for healing on the Sabbath. The rules say that Sabbath, as a gift from God, is a time set aside to rest, celebrate, enjoy, and use in God's honor. Jesus reminds his critics that "the Sabbath is made for humankind, not humankind for the Sabbath" (verse 27). If we turn the Sabbath into one more excuse for rule orientation and fault finding, we have surely misused the gift.

Wise leaders understand and accept the rules but are also willing to break them if they have good reasons. For example, are the rules hurting someone? Are they keeping the job from getting done? Are they preventing the greater good? This is a hard lesson for the *order* people, but nobody needs to hear it more than they do.

As you consider your own style of leadership, do you think you might be spending too much time enforcing a set of obsolete rules? When we're too critical and judgmental, we can hurt others and ourselves. Are you quite sure you're right and those who disagree with you are wrong? Are you allowing your employees or the group you lead to stay open and creative to the possibility of change? Do they understand that the rules may have to bend when there's a really good reason? Have you found ways to convince them when there's a need for change? In the end, the *order* people may not understand. Still there are times when you'll have to find the courage to go forward anyway.

Good Leaders

- understand there are exceptions to most every rule;
- are willing to admit they may be wrong;
- don't turn their leadership into a strict set of rules;
- know that, sometimes, the rules must be broken in order to make things work.

LET THE DEAD BURY THE DEAD (MATT 8:21-22, LUKE 9:59-62): JESUS GIVES AN URGENT MESSAGE

Some people see the New Testament as grace-filled and the Hebrew Scripture (Old Testament) as only filled with little more than judgment and wrath. Actually, the Hebrew Scripture is also filled with grace. For an example, look at what happens in Deut 20:5-9 when there's a need to go to battle with enemies and troops are being mustered. Under certain circumstances, the soldier is permitted to stay back and is not required to go with the others into battle. These circumstances are listed. One may stay back from going to battle for the following reasons: (1) to dedicate a new house, (2) to enjoy the fruits of any vineyard he may have planted but not yet enjoyed, (3) to consummate a marriage, and (4) if he is afraid, because he might dishearten his fellow soldiers with such an attitude. Most of the above reasons for staying back from battle were vital to meet the needs of ancient Jewish people. The consummation of marriage was required to perpetuate the nation. The planting of one's field would have been needed to feed one's family's needs and, as an adjunct, also to help the poor with what produce was left over.

Today we may not literally have to stay out of battle to plant our field. Are we in some ways like the person who was allowed to stay behind? Are we at times simply unable to move into new realms or new possibilities? Then, it is best we wait. The Hebrew Scriptures used a battle scenario, probably for good reason. What life will be like in the days ahead is always somewhat unknown and is very likely to include at least some dangers and difficulties. The battle leaders in the Hebrew Scripture knew what they were doing when they chose not to send certain people into war at certain times. A soldier who is unable to concentrate on the battle because of distractions related to issues back home is not going to be the best kind of fighter, comrade, or protector! Others can do the job until that one is ready.

Strangely, the New Testament often proves more demanding than the Hebrew Scripture. In Matthew, a man wants to follow Jesus and asks if he can just go back home to bury his father; Jesus surprisingly does not say yes. He tells him instead, "Follow me, and let the dead bury their own dead" (Matt 8:22). And in the version of this same story from the Gospel of Luke, Jesus adds, "But as for you, go and proclaim the kingdom of God" (Luke 9:60b). In Luke, another example is offered when a second person says to Jesus, "I will follow you, Lord; but let me first say farewell to those at my home" (Luke 9:61). Jesus' response seems harsh by our standards when he replies, "No one who puts a hand to the plow and looks back is fit for the kingdom of God" (Luke 9:62). These are strong words! The point is to show us that times had changed, and Jesus' message now must be that there are no excuses at all; the proverbial time is now! The emergence of God's reign is no longer just a future hope or dream; it is imminent. Watchfulness and readiness are required from all concerned, no matter what else is going on in their lives. Nothing, absolutely nothing, is to hold them back.

We may, at first, find Jesus is demanding much more than we think anyone can bear. We have every excuse not to do the work of loving our neighbor, caring for the poor, fighting evil, and seeking peace. It is so much easier for us to complain about the times we live in, plan to do something about it later, and keep busy with the status quo than to find ourselves ready to lay claim to new possibilities in our own time. After all, who has time today, for example, to protest bad legislation or fight injustice? Who has time to help at a food pantry? Isn't it easier not to get involved in working to bring about systemic change or to make our workplaces and businesses places of genuine honesty and justice? We may not have a parent to bury, but we often have reasons to avoid making change for the better. Modern lives are so demanding. Our families come first. We have responsibilities. The list of our own excuses goes on. Yet the fact is that, even today, Jesus' message is valid and vital. The time to put away excuses, however valid they may seem, is always right now, and we are still today being challenged to drop everything else and move forward.

Good Leaders

- know there are times to hold back and times to reach and stretch forward;
- realize that some of their very best excuses are exactly that: excuses!

THE PRICES WE PAY (LUKE 14:25-33): THE COST CAN BE HIGH

Today's leaders cannot help but notice the continuing rise in prices. We ask ourselves how much we are willing to pay for needed items.

To make those decisions, we must consider how important each item is to us or our business or group. What material things in life do you want or need the most? And how much are you willing to pay for them? What in life that is not material do you desire the most? What do you want the most for the business you manage or the people you lead? Now, how much of yourself, your time, and your assets are you willing to pay for that?

We are careful about the prices we pay when it comes to spending our money. But Jesus talks about some of the bigger prices and the more important things. Have you ever thought about the price you may have paid for some things such as the decisions you have made? For example, what about a job you didn't take for whatever reason—a job that may have led to another and then to what might have been all kinds of money and security or fame and fortune? Many leaders think they have paid those kinds of prices. But were there also good things that happened because of a decision you might have made *not* to take the job? Also, what about a relationship or a partnership that did not happen because, at a particular moment in time, you chose not to get involved?

And then there are the prices we pay for our good deeds, for doing what's right. It's a well-kept secret because we don't want to discourage people, but it may be quite true, as the old joke says, "No good deed goes unpunished." At the very least, we don't always get the rewards we might have expected for doing the right thing. The sad truth is that people do not always "do to us" as we have "done to them"!

Often people will join up with a group not realizing what they're getting into, not checking into or really thinking about the real cost of it. Jesus tries to help the crowds understand that if they want to follow him, they'll have to be willing to give up a lot. They're going to have to make a commitment with their whole hearts. He even says that to follow him, people will have to be willing to "hate father and mother, wife and children, brothers and sisters" (verse 26). Wait a minute! What about "family values"? (In a recent television commercial, a schoolteacher says something like this to a young woman, "The trouble with you kids is that you've got no values." The young woman's response is, "What do you mean? I tell you, I got this blouse I'm wearing for fifteen dollars at Rob's Department Store. Now that's value!) Similarly, taken literally, who could understand any requirement that we hate our mother and father? Family loyalty is revered in our culture and rightly so, for it's of primary importance. Jesus is making a strong point here. It's not that Jesus literally wants his followers to hate their families. But he's making it clear that if they're going to follow him and do what they think is right, even their own families might disown them. Their first commitment must be toward the things of God not the things of humankind. Jesus is pushing the envelope to make them think about what price they're willing to pay to follow him.

Next, he tries another tactic, this time closer to the business mode. If you're going to build a tower, he says, you'll need to estimate the cost in advance to be sure that you'll have enough money to finish the job (verse 28). Again, before you get started on any project, you know as a leader that you'll need to ask yourself whether you're willing to see it through to the end of the project, whatever the cost.

Jesus continues with a final example. If you were a king going to war, you'd have to keep in mind that if you have ten thousand men and the other king has twenty thousand, you aren't likely to win the battle (verse 31). As we know too well, once a nation has committed to engage in a war, it's very likely the other side will retaliate or, at very least, defend itself. War, like pregnancy, is not something you can just undo. You have to ask yourself in advance what price you're willing to pay.

Jesus is pointing out one practical fact that so many leaders don't like to face. It is that we must be responsible for both the cost and the results of the decisions we make. Sometimes good people get a raw deal. But, as wonderful as they may be as people, there's something they don't always understand. Life has never been a guaranteed fifty-fifty proposition. Jesus calls his leaders, and all people, to follow the way of good, and there's a price to pay for every stance we take. Leaders need to accept that fact and move forward. Maybe we'll lose something we hold dear when we choose the right road. Also, we won't necessarily even be rewarded for the good we do. But we do it anyway. Think of all the people you know who've done what is right! They didn't do it for a reward. They did it for love and because it was right.

We all remember the words of the late President John Kennedy when he spoke about what you can do for your country. Jesus is giving the religious version, suggesting, "Think not what the people you lead can do for you, but what, together, you can do for your people, and for this troubled world." Nobody promised that leadership would be easy or that the world would be without troubles. But as a leader, you can be a part of change for the good. In his book *The Contrarian's Guide to Leadership*, Steven B. Sample lists principles for a leader to break free from the ordinary. In his list of fourteen principles, one is this: "We should know what hill we are willing to die on."[1] Hopefully we'll be able to do what is right without dying.

Good Leaders

- understand there's a cost for right decisions and good leadership;
- do not always expect a fifty-fifty proposition;
- choose to do good anyway, even when things are not going their way;
- have decided in advance what they are willing to "die" for.

DRESS FOR THE PARTY (MATT 22:1–14): BEING RESPECTFUL OF THE OCCASION

Leadership suffers when leaders see themselves as not having enough of what they need to get the job done. This may apply to money, materials, or even followers. Too often, however, it is the

1. Sample, *Contrarian's Guide*, 112.

perception of lack rather than the fact of it that gets in the way. How can you, as a leader, find the confidence to really believe and know all your needs will be met?

Jesus tells this strange story. A person is giving a big party and invites all the appropriate people. They don't respond. So, discouraged, he decides to send his servants out into the street to invite everyone they can find, "both good and bad" (verse 10). So far so good! The strangeness of this story really begins when one person from the street shows up at the party, and then he gets thrown out because it is decided that he is not properly attired for attending an event such as this! What can such an "off the wall" story possibly teach us about leadership? After all, if the man was invited in, shouldn't he have been accepted in the clothes he was wearing and not have been expected to appear in appropriate clothing—namely, some kind of wedding robe (verse 11)? Clearly, he had not gone out into the street with any plans to be attending a wedding. Why was he now expected to suddenly be decked out in his best clothes?

In general, a parable has only one point, and it's not acceptable to push parables beyond that main point. But, what's the point here? We do not have to be dressed to the hilt in order to be invited into the banquet that life can be. Still, once we accept the invitation, we're required to participate fully and joyfully. Once we've entered God's grace, we're already, in effect, "at the party," and it just won't work if we choose to carry on as we were before. There is a new responsibility on our part to respond appropriately. This parable, needless to say, is neither about parties nor party clothes but about our opportunities to change for the better, and about the choices we make when these opportunities present themselves. Once we realize we are, indeed, at the banquet, how then can we remain in any kind of state of spiritual poverty?

New clothing in this parable represents the new you! Once life and leadership are viewed as a banquet, how can we see ourselves as poor? People who recognize they're at the banquet will see themselves open to new chances, better ideas, and alternative solutions. The gift of life as a banquet has already been given. All we must do is recognize that we've been invited and then see to it that we are truly present and looking good!

Good Leaders

- see life as a banquet and never think of themselves as poor;
- accept the invitation and rise to the occasion;
- know if they don't change on the inside, they're still standing outside the banquet door in their old clothes.

THE TIME IS NOW (LUKE 4:14-21): JESUS INTERPRETS SCRIPTURE

Too often leaders think they have to wait until all the pieces are in place, all the conditions met, and all the assets lined up before they can move ahead. They don't realize the "appointed time" is always now.

Jesus is called up to read Scripture in the synagogue on the Sabbath. He stands up and reads from the book of the prophet Isaiah, saying, "The Spirit of the Lord is upon me, because he has anointed me to bring good news to the poor. He has sent me to proclaim release to the captives and recovery of sight to the blind, to set free those who are oppressed, to proclaim the year of the Lord's favor" (Luke 4:18-19). And then he adds some startling words of his own that shock his listeners. He adds, "This scripture has been fulfilled in your hearing" (verse 21b). The usual sermon or scholarly comment on this passage suggests that Jesus is offering these added words to let the people know he is the expected Messiah and that they should recognize him as God's chosen one. This may be so, but we can see too that Jesus is also giving some very practical advice. He is pointing out that the time to do God's will is not tomorrow, not some time in the future, but right now: today. The congregation responds by becoming so angry with Jesus that they try to throw him off the nearest cliff. Assuredly, there have been many instances since that time when a congregation, after hearing a new young pastor's sermon, wanted to throw that pastor off the nearest cliff! But seriously, people often do become angry when they hear this kind of truth. Jesus may indeed have been proclaiming himself the chosen one, but he was also telling the listeners to stop waiting for tomorrow because the time that counts is right now.

How willing are we as leaders to really get on with our lives? When will we be willing to stop being overly cautious and truly make ourselves present "in the moment"? Leaders often get so busy making plans for tomorrow that they miss today!

Good Leaders

- are aware of what needs to be done and deal with it now, not later;
- recognize today as the "appointed time";
- know the world can change for the better right now and are ready to be a part of it.

Conclusion

THIS BOOK HAS TOUCHED upon just some of the leadership methods taught and employed by Jesus, as we understand him through the four Gospel accounts. Although millions in this world proclaim themselves to be Christians, many of these same people are quick to admit that Jesus presents them with some big challenges. Some may even secretly think the ways of Jesus to be perfect in principle but less than practical for a CEO or other leader in today's world. This book has been written to help those who would be leaders. It also demonstrates that Jesus never backed away from courageous leadership. Jesus continually and consistently manifested great leadership in his life and was always both courageous and forthright in his teachings. The leadership lessons offered here, far from being out-of-date, have proven to be vital for good leadership even in the complex and diverse situations in which we now work and live. The preceding chapters have demonstrated a plethora of good leadership examples and real ways we as leaders, at whatever level, can follow his example.

These times we live in can be trying times for leaders. Perhaps you chose this book because you were looking for useful practical leadership tips and methods. Are you feeling more courageous now? You may have opened this book because you were seeking to improve in your role as a leader. Maybe you already see yourself as a good leader and were looking for reinforcement. It is hoped that you have found some useful ideas for leadership from the great teachings and actions of the greatest leader of all.

A PROFILE OF COURAGEOUS LEADERS

Here is a short description of courageous leaders gleaned from the Jesus stories we have studied here. Courageous leaders are not necessarily fearless. They are not fools, so they don't go looking for trouble. Still, they have a strong sense of who they are and where they stand in the scheme of things. These leaders make the best of a situation, not just for themselves but for everyone involved. They have no desire to be pandered to and are always more interested in understanding the reality of a given situation than in closing their eyes to it. They are willing to sacrifice in order to have a good life, and when and if they do get such a life, they're willing and anxious to share the good with others. Courageous leaders keep aware of what they do and how it affects those around them. These leaders are seekers of peace, but not at all costs. They know that peace is no peace without justice. They seek to say yes but are not afraid to say no. Courageous leaders, in the end, are ordinary people who, in the face of the challenges of life, are often surprised to find themselves behaving in ways that are quite extraordinary.

Ultimately, the courage we find for leadership need not even be our own. People of faith believe that they are not ultimately alone, that God is with us, around us uplifting, behind us prodding, and in front of us beckoning. In his life and teachings, Jesus was always a great leader. In his passion and crucifixion, he proved himself the consummate role model for courageous leadership. In the simplest of Jesus' statements, "Follow me," we are invited to follow him by serving others through our own leadership. Here are his simple words to Peter, whom he chose to be his primary disciple: "Feed my lambs. . . . Tend my sheep. . . . Feed my sheep"

Conclusion

(John 21:15–17). In the end, every kind of leadership is exactly that, doing for others. How can we do otherwise?

This book has not been specifically geared toward showing leaders how we can make a better world but, in the end, it comes down to that. If we are working in the ways we've seen Jesus work, then whether we are doing it intentionally or not, we are participating in much more than making a success for ourselves. We are also in some small way bringing about justice, peace, equality, and helping others enjoy more fruitful lives. In the end, what all of us want is to feel we've done our part and that our labor and leadership have not been in vain. However eager our intentions, and however diligent our work as leaders, just as we suspected at the outset, we are not likely to become just like Jesus. Rather, Jesus stands before all of us as the consummate role model. His words and actions present a goal toward which we can strive. Jesus is, indeed, a courageous leader and certainly he is the best CEO. We have our marching orders!

Bibliography

Davies, W. D., and Dale C. Allison Jr. *Introduction and Commentary on Matthew I–VII*. Vol. 1 of *The Gospel According to Saint Matthew*. International Critical Commentary. Edinburgh: T&T Clark, 1988.
Pagels, Elaine. *The Origin of Satan*. New York: Random House, 1995.
Prete, Anthony. "Shalom: Much More than Peace." Friends Journal, Nov. 1, 2003. https://www.friendsjournal.org/2003133/.
Sample, Stephen B. *The Contrarian's Guide to Leadership*. San Francisco: Jossey-Bass, 2002.

www.ingramcontent.com/pod-product-compliance
Lightning Source LLC
Chambersburg PA
CBHW070920180426
43192CB00038B/1977